TAKE BACK THE REMOTE CONTROL IN YOUR LIFE

STAY
TUNED

BALANCING FAITH, FAMILY AND CAREER
WITHOUT COMPROMISING YOU

FOREWORD BY BISHOP PAUL S. MORTON

NICK F. NELSON

PARAMIND PUBLICATIONS
A *Shift* in Thinking

ParaMind Publications

Copyright © 2016 by Nick F. Nelson
Published by ParaMind Publications

Library of Congress Control Number: 2016914238
ISBN 978-0-9979870-0-3
Printed in the United States of America

DEDICATION

For Tiffany and Quinn. You are my why.
I love you.

Channel Guide

FOREWORD

In the Marketing industry, Nick F. Nelson is one of the premier leaders, especially in Brand Management. In this new, exciting, and timely book, "Stay Tuned," Nick penned some valuable lessons to help enlighten, encourage and strengthen his readers. In today's world of literature, there are so many books geared toward self-help, motivation, and self-discovery. Nick's book is refreshing because it goes beyond a simple "how to," and shares real life experiences that the average reader can relate to and glean important keys for success.

"Stay Tuned" has set a high bar as it relates to sharing with readers elements to help them not just tune into their careers but also make sure they stay tuned into the most important aspect of life, and that's FAMILY.

Nick's transparency about his balancing act in pursuit of a successful career is priceless. I urge you to grab hold of the life-changing words, gain wisdom, utilize his insight, and make good use of the practical tools as they leap off the pages of this powerful book. May you find peace, purpose and increase your spiritual connection with God on your journey to success.

Bishop Paul S. Morton Sr.
Founder, Full Gospel Baptist Church
Fellowship International
Senior Pastor, Changing a Generation Ministries,
Atlanta, Georgia

UPFRONTS

C an you remember that high-pitched skirling sound you would hear during the pre-cable era when the TV would go off the air at around midnight or so? The format varied little from station to station across the country. First, a few technical details were announced, then a reading of "High Flight" followed by the national anthem, and then the steady high-pitched beeeeeeeeeeeeeep tone of the test pattern. In addition to signaling the end of another broadcasting day, I believe that long unnerving tone was also created to wake people up who had fallen asleep sitting in front of the TV, so they could get up and turn it off.

Many of us need that beeeeeeeeeeeeeep back in our lives today, figuratively, because we've fallen asleep. We've disconnected and tuned out life. Have you found yourself locked on autopilot maintaining your status quo or veering further off course because you have no clue how to get and stay tuned in? Well, guess what? You're not alone.

1

My name is Nick F. Nelson, a man of God, dedicated husband to my wife, Tiffany Avery-Nelson, and father to my son, Quinn. Professionally, I am an entertainment marketing executive. As the Chief Marketing Officer (CMO) and owner of LIQUID SOUL, the nation's premier strategic communications agency for entertainment and consumer brands, part of my job is to get people to tune in — tune into a TV show, engage with a brand, or go to the movies on a particular date at a specific time. It requires me to be very proactive, intentional, and resourceful and to leverage relationships, all in an attempt to get people's attention.

Over the past decade, I've attained success marketing some of the most acclaimed films and television projects in the industry. Getting to this point in my career has not been easy and at various points along the way, the job has had a negative impact on both my family and personal life. Being in an industry that moves at such a fast pace, I found myself so focused on the next project that I never really appreciated the now — that is until 2013.

In 2013, I lost both my father, William E. Nelson Jr. (due to complications with diabetes and kidney failure), and my spiritual father and pastor, W. Ron Sailor Sr., whose unexpected death came as a result of chronic health issues. When those tragic losses happened, it hurt. Yet, I had to press on because I still had to address business issues, personal responsibilities at home, and manage the care of my mother, Della, who suffers from Alzheimer's disease.

Experiencing the loss of these men caused my life's lens to change. This is because for the first time, I didn't have a man to go to who truly knew me, would listen and could offer wise counsel without being critical or judgmental. Although I had Tiffany, other family, and a few friends, I still felt like I was alone and teetering toward the breaking point.

Since that time, I've gone through a healing process that has caused me to take a tough look at myself, make necessary life adjustments, and reflect on some of the lessons my mentors tried to teach me. Through this book, I want to share some of what I learned with you, in the hopes that perhaps you can avoid the pitfalls that have nearly derailed me along the way.

The common thread of the life lessons I've learned is that your faith, family, and personal well-being cannot be compromised for your career and the pursuit of "stuff."

My father and pastor wanted me to stay tuned and find purpose in my work; however, they did not want my work life to be more important to me than my family or personal well-being.

STAY TUNED is a self-help guide for professional men and the women that support them. It's targeted toward those men seeking to achieve work-life balance so that they may have time to recognize and focus on those things that matter most in life.

This is not to say that I have all the answers, but I do have perspective from the wisdom I received and the lessons I've learned through the mistakes I've made. The experiences shared in these pages and the takeaways at the end of each chapter will help you take back the remote control in your life. In order to succeed, you must be proactive and get your own attention. You have to wake yourself up and say:

"You know what? I cannot go through life sleepwalking, assuming that everything will take care of itself. I have to recognize when things are out of balance and that adjustments need to be made, and I can't be afraid to make them."

After years of succeeding professionally and failing personally, I've learned that maintaining balance and being present is the key to living a happy and healthy life. I call this staying tuned.

If I had stayed tuned I would have seen the danger signs in advance and been aware. We fail in life because we don't pay attention to the signs. We're accustomed to a routine, so we lose our footing when things change, and that often causes us to lose our way.

We don't attempt to improve ourselves because in our own way we think we have everything under control; but in reality, we find ourselves off balance, not prioritizing effectively, and putting more emphasis on things that are fleeting rather than things of substance that can add value to our lives. We say we're good but inside, we're teetering on the brink of losing what matters most, trying to hold on to things that aren't that important in the grand scheme of life.

Through my company LIQUID SOUL, I've been successful in getting people to tune in to any number of film and television projects. However, with this book, it is my desire to share my experiences, which I hope will shed some light on how to tune into your life.

This book is a huge step for me as I share the process that helped me overcome myself and find that oh-so-elusive footing that allows me to balance. I've never considered myself a writer. This is because in order to be a writer, you must have a clear understanding of the English language, which I occasionally struggle with. Nonetheless, I'm still giving this a shot because I believe a part of my purpose is to inform and inspire others by being transparent and real. You see, I've never been one to let my flaws get in my way, and I'm surely not about to start now.

What I'm sharing with you is the reinvention and discovery of Nick F. Nelson. Just like any great product, there have been many versions of me over the years. Think about it: Apple is always working to build the next best iteration of the iPhone to ensure that it's meeting the needs of the people that invest in it. If a billion dollar company like Apple finds it necessary to continue to reinvent itself, why wouldn't you continue to make sure that you're creating the best version of you?

If you are a professional male who is ready to establish balance between your faith, family, and career while staying tuned in to your life, this book is for you. STAY TUNED is a compilation of personal stories. It is designed to help you achieve a different perspective on your life and inspire you to calibrate yourself, so you can tune in.

In the television industry, in May of every year, various broadcast networks host Upfronts. These are events where the networks provide a sneak peek of their fall program lineup to advertisers in hopes that they will place buys upfront at a discounted rate. Well, if you are reading this book, you have paid your price of admission; or, at the very least, someone else has paid it for you. If you're ready to tune in to your life, surf this book's 10 channels and discover the stories and solutions that serve as my guide to staying tuned.

You've been watching your life unfold; and now, the Star Spangled Banner is playing while the beep isn't far behind. It's time to wake up. Wake up your mind from the half-truths and distractions that have many of us missing the real point to our lives and therefore, not nurturing what truly matters. It all begins with you, so if something is going to change, you must be the one to change it. Please, accept what you can learn from my experiences, and know that I share them in the hopes that they encourage you to take back the remote control in your life. The time for change is now. You can do it.

STAY TUNED

Nick F. Nelson

Stay Tuned

Channel One

IT STARTS WITH ME

The star of your own show

Growing up as an only child, I spent quite a bit of time alone at home with my mother, who was very protective of me, and my father, who traveled regularly. During my alone time, although my main creative outlet was music and writing, television was my favorite form of entertainment. It was a constant companion that shaped my worldview and played a big role in my development, influencing me to this day. Shows like "Different Strokes," "The Fresh Prince of Bel-Air," "A Different World," and others exposed me to a world that I never knew existed. One that was exciting and edgy, yet cool.

Unlike the shows we see on TV, however, life is real, unscripted, and does not always leave time for a commercial break. In life, we are the star of our own show, and the question we must ask ourselves is, "What role I am playing?"

Far too often, we allow others to direct our life story instead of making the calls ourselves. We allow others to sit in the director's chair, thus giving them complete creative control to define us or tell us who we are on cue. I know this all too well because I've spent a good portion of my life allowing others to define me, trying my best to remember my lines and act out the parts. For years, I heard, "You're Dr. Nelson's son (my father had a PhD in political science)," or "You're Big Nick (a name given to me in college because of my size at the time)," or, "You're that LIQUID SOUL Guy." I had to learn to tell myself, "No, those are just pieces of me. I'm bigger than those titles." I decided to take back the remote by looking in the mirror, saying, "I am Nick F. Nelson and I am perfect even in all my imperfections."

Made from experience

Many people call themselves experts. Some are relationship experts, financial experts, coaches, etc. I'm none of that. I do not hold a degree in psychology or human behavior, so I don't want to position myself as such. What I can speak about or relate to are the challenges of rediscovering ourselves and developing into whom and what God wants us to be. I can speak on the challenges of identifying one's overall purpose and how to get there. I can talk about how we should challenge ourselves to develop our self-worth and value that helps us find out who we are — and then begin to love ourselves. I've made some mistakes and have a few regrets, but they have helped build me into the person I am, and I'm happy being him today.

My experiences give me the authority because I have lived through them. It's inauthentic to speak on things we haven't lived firsthand: confidence, relationship, marriage, family, money and business issues. I've had them. I've been successful and I've failed, but there's something about living and overcoming the thing that has the potential to destroy us, and that makes us stronger when we face it head on. These failures motivate me to share aspects of my journey with others. I believe I can help someone by pointing out the places in the road where the manhole cover was missing — where I fell in and climbed back out.

For example, when I first became a father, I had no idea how to do it. I didn't know how to feed, burp, hold, or get my son on a schedule. I had to learn it through trial and error, and by asking others, including my wife, Tiffany, who knew much more than I did in this area. After seeking wise counsel, I received great advice that helped me get it right.

Don't get me wrong, I'm still learning and searching, but I've grown — growth that is evident in my walk. I never professed to know it all, and I'm far from being perfect. I may even sound hypocritical at times because I may not always take my own advice. Not because it's not valuable or I don't believe that it works but, rather, because I am human.

Watch out for signs

Many times in life, we fail because we don't pay attention to the signs. The American Traffic Solutions organization reported that from 2007-2011, an average of 751 people died each year in red-light-running crashes. This means someone wasn't paying attention to the signs, and the consequence was death. Sure, all the consequences you may face from inattention will not be fatal; but they could cause harm, setbacks, and challenges that could have been avoided if only you had stayed tuned in.

Ask yourself, "Have I been missing signs?" "Could not paying attention to the signs be the reason why I have fallen short or failed in the past?" What has been your main challenge? In my case, my failures came as a result of me tuning out. The signs were staring me in the face and I chose to ignore them. If I had stayed tuned in, I would have recognized the signs, and I could have chosen to follow them.

The God connection

My challenges have helped to increase my overall faith. God's tests are designed to remind us of God's power and grace. As long as we live, there will be things for us to figure out. When you understand this, you become less cocky and more open to learn. Problems often arise because we don't know what we don't know; yet we act as if we have all the answers or as if we have it all together, but we don't. It's okay to say you don't know. The key is to decide not to remain in a state of ignorance but instead find the best way to get to a solution.

You must have a plan for your life and set real goals that become your story line as you act it out. You must recap often to get a good view of your story to ensure you don't rerun the failures but instead continue to launch new shows that create the ratings you desire. In life, it's critical to know the answer to questions such as, "Who am I?" and "What's my purpose?" You need to assess what you are doing and your value. To have any success, you must have answers to these questions to begin to find your balance and peace. These answers come from God.

I have learned that in order to play my role in life, I need to maintain my connection with God. It's been those times in my life when I stopped talking to Him and stopped seeking His guidance and listening to His voice that were most challenging for me.

Establishing and maintaining your connection with God is critical if you desire to establish balance in your life and walk in your purpose. As we connect with God, we learn how to conduct ourselves — considering the importance of morals and morality — and that tomorrow isn't promised and that today is all we have to get it right. We understand that death is a part — and, of course, the end-point — of the process, and thus the fear of it will be removed when we have the right perspective about life. This does not mean that we won't be sad or hurt when a loved one dies; but we will accept that death is a part of His divine process.

Your presence is a gift

Do you remember a time when families sat down and ate dinner together? If you don't, believe it or not, you are not alone. Increased work demands, combined with our dependency on technology to stay connected, have given many of us a 24/7/365 mentality to think it's natural and right to respond to work-related items day or night.

This desire to stay connected has caused us to be disconnected from others. And what suffers the most? The family. According to a 2015 survey of 2,000+ working adults, from cloud-based enterprise workforce management solution provider Workfront, 38 percent of employees have missed life events because of bad work-life balance. The fact is that our families are being neglected because too many times we take more pride in being available to our career than being available to our family.

In 2010, after my company won our largest account as an agency to that point, I began falling into that cycle. I remember one day "checking in" to one of my social media applications at an airport after boarding a flight, and I received a notification saying, "Congratulations! You've been in airports five weeks in a row."

Social media was celebrating me because I'd been flying across the country, even though I was disconnected from my family. Instead of that being a cause for celebration, it should have been a cause for concern. I should have gotten a notification with alarm bells ringing off the hook, reminding me to evaluate what success looks like.

The amount of success or failure you experience in life begins with looking in the mirror. You are the reason for your abundance or lack of progress to this point in your life. Remember that your presence, and being present in the life of those family members and friends that you love, is the most amazing gift you could ever give them. If you choose not to give it, that's on you. Just bear in mind that the balance and peace we have in life is a direct result of our decisions. And our decisions are the products of our thoughts.

The responsibility for your life resides within you. Therefore, if your life is off balance and peace seems to elude you, you have to examine your beliefs and your actions. When I decided to take control of my life, I made the decision to prioritize my personal happiness and my family, not my church, not my job, nor my many community obligations. I decided to seek peace first; and for me, peace is making sure that those foundational things in my life are solid. Once that's in place, I can build everything else from there.

Removing the mask

The questions "Who am I?" and "What am I doing?" force us to be honest with ourselves. They require us to identify certain critical areas like where we need to improve, where we've failed, what strengths we have and what we're passionate about. Most people fall short in the process of self-examination because they don't dig deep and do the work it takes to make such an essential self-discovery. They are afraid, and maybe they don't know how to go about it or just don't want to do it.

As the star of our own show, we all play many roles in life. I am a husband, father, son, caregiver, entrepreneur, manager, mentor, and community and faith leader. Each role means something different and requires different parts of me to be effective or successful.

To effectively carry out each role, I had to take an honest assessment of me — my whole being and life — and remove the mask that used to hide my true self. The mask concept has always stuck with me because it rings so true. We all wear some type of mask. We might fake it until we make it at work or act as if we know what we're doing as parents and in other relationships or other situations where we are clueless. We want people to believe that we know it, so we put on a facade. It's okay not to know but not okay not to learn.

A huge part of the challenge we often face is we don't know who we are. While pledging the Beta Nu Chapter of Alpha Phi Alpha at Florida A&M University (FAMU), I had to learn a poem, which had a profound effect on me. The poem was Paul Laurence Dunbar's "We Wear the Mask." Dunbar was a scholar and one of the first African-American poets to gain national recognition. Dunbar wrote:

We wear the mask that grins and lies,
It hides our cheeks and shades our eyes,—
This debt we pay to human guile;
With torn and bleeding hearts, we smile
And mouth with myriad subtleties,
Why should the world be over-wise,
In counting all our tears and sighs?
Nay, let them only see us, while

Nick F. Nelson

> **We wear the mask.**
>
> **We smile, but oh great Christ, our cries**
>
> **To thee from tortured souls arise.**
> **We sing, but oh the clay is vile**
> **Beneath our feet, and long the mile,**
> **But let the world dream otherwise,**
> **We wear the mask!**

You might be able to (or even need to) play the front and wear a mask with other people, but you can't wear a mask with yourself.

On the path to finding our purpose and taking action, we must take inventory of ourselves. This is achieved by identifying our gifts and talents. By determining what needs to be improved and listening to God, because He is always talking; we just have to be in tune to hear Him. We must be obedient and intentional to take action. This action pushes us to make strides forward.

Walking by faith rather than sight means that even when we don't know or understand how it's going to happen, we're confident that it will happen. I've learned that I can't be scared of the unknown and have to push forward. Hebrews 11:1 reminds us that, "Faith is the substance of things hoped for and the evidence of things not seen." In order to activate this faith, we must understand that faith and fear cannot coexist.

Anything you desire, want to change, or accomplish begins with you. By knowing yourself and understanding the buck starts and stops with you, you're able to assess your situation and create an informed plan of action to tune in.

Why we should stay tuned

If you take nothing else from this book, it is my hope that you walk away with an attitude of not wallowing in regrets or fretting about the future, but that you instead determine to live in the now by being present.

To "stay tuned" means waking up and realizing that in order to succeed in life, you must live in the present. I learned long ago that showing up is the first step, but when you show up, you must be alert and engaged. By doing this, you will be amazed at the peace you feel in all areas of your life. It's a simple formula but not always easy to accomplish.

In 2013, after experiencing my losses, I began to reflect on what my father and my pastor were trying to tell me. My dad was a highly respected political scientist and one of the founding fathers of the "black studies" movement. His career afforded him the opportunity to travel all over the world; however, before his death, he told me he deeply regretted not spending enough time with his family. My pastor was a highly acclaimed media personality, but despite all of the awards and acclaim, he passed away at an early age. His heath issues had compounded over the years, and he could not resolve them even though he tried.

They were both great men, doing great things, but it often seems that great men doing great things have personal traumatizing issues. For example, Marvin Gaye was a musical genius, but he had all sorts of family issues. Johnnie Cochran was a wonderful lawyer with allegedly two different families, and the list continues of both men and women who were great professionally but stumbled in their personal lives.

Your career may be intact, but that's not what's most important at the end of the day. When it's your time to say bye to this world, your career will not be at your deathbed. What you want is to have your family and your faith beside you. Those are the two things that I encourage you to embrace before you leave this earth.

STAY TUNED TAKEAWAYS

- Be the star of your own show by knowing your role and respecting your cast mates.

- Let your life experiences propel you forward, not push you back.

- Don't be a "know it all," be a "learn it all."

- Pay attention to life's signs. They provide direction and help avoid unnecessary collisions.

- Set boundaries around your personal life. Understand that there are places you should not go and people you should not let in.

- Take your mask off. Be transparent and your life will be transformational.

IF I'M NOT HAPPY

What happiness is

Happiness is an emotion that comes from within. It can be found in the present by making peace with the past and looking forward in expectation toward the future.

Happiness is intangible. We can't put it in our pocket and save it for later. I've learned that if I'm not happy but seeking happiness, I must first look inside of myself to determine what's preventing me from finding it.

Happiness is purpose. At one point my life was task-driven and lacked real purpose. Finding happiness is bigger than completing the things on my to-do list; it's more about being present and engaged.

Happiness is intentional and genuine. You cannot fake happiness. Rather, happiness is real when you wake up each morning and you are at peace.

Happiness is peace. If I'm not at peace, my mental health and mental well-being are not intact. I've been in so many situations where I didn't have peace; and when I didn't have peace in my spirit, my soul was not at rest — and it showed in everything I did.

One example I can recall is shortly after Tiffany and were married and had settled in Atlanta. She persuaded me for the first time in years to attend church regularly. Tiffany has always been a strong woman of faith and encouraged me to work on my relationship with the Lord, so that I might properly position myself as head of our household.

Ironically at the time we both worked for the same company, in the same department. One day a colleague invited us to attend her church, Christ The King Baptist, located in Dacula, GA, a tiny city north of Atlanta. This is when I met Bishop W. Ron Sailor Sr. I can recall his presence was massive. He was a big man with an even bigger personality. After attending the church for some time, my wife was ready to join. I was still on the fence because I was not quite ready to commit to church every week. After several weeks had passed she appealed to me a final time to make a commitment to join. She told me that she did not want to make this move alone but would if she had to because she could no longer neglect the direction the Lord had placed on her heart. I surely did not want her to make such an important move without me, so I said yes, and we walked down that aisle together the following Sunday. Today not only are we still members but work as ministry leaders together.

After I joined Christ The King, although I was in the service, I wasn't necessarily into "church." By the time service was over and I hit the door, I was off to the next thing that may not have been quite "church-like." This became my routine, but I wasn't at peace. I was just going through the motions. I wasn't at peace because I wasn't happy, and I wasn't happy because I was not at peace. My unhappiness had nothing to do with my wife, my friends, or even my job, for that matter. In reality, I just wasn't happy with me. I felt that I was not equipped to handle the challenges of being a spouse and leader in my home. My 'fake it until you make it' strategy was wearing me away; and for the first time in life, I had to stand up and be a man.

Happiness is not only hard to measure, but it is also difficult to singularly define. We can't define happiness without using a synonym for happiness, and we can't interpret it to everyone's satisfaction.

Defining happiness might be easier if we take a moment to remember those times in life in which we were the happiest.

I remember being truly happy when:
- Mom made her famous catfish dinner on Friday nights.

- I spent Saturdays with Dad going to breakfast, the movies, roller skating, or to The Ohio State University football games.

- My first clique gelled my sophomore year of high school after I'd spent the year before getting teased because of my weight.

- I pledged Alpha Phi Alpha, Beta Nu chapter, with 16 other guys who became not only my line brothers but my friends for life.

- I graduated from The Ohio State University and proved to myself that I was intelligent, establishing lifelong friendships along the way.

- I received confirmation from God, while flying for work, that I had found my helpmeet in Tiffany and the day I made her my wife.

- My business partner and I chased after new opportunities and dreamed big about new ways to expand our territory.

- Tiffany and I held our baby boy (whom we had waited almost eight years to have) for the very first time.

While growing from childhood to adulthood, happiness has meant different things to me, and this concept continues to evolve. What makes me happy today is to have balance and peace in my life. I'm not talking about false peace, but that genuine peace that comes with walking in my truth and being the person that I was created to be. That type of happiness is contagious, and my desire is to make sure it permeates my spirit daily.

The three dimensions of happiness

According to Martin Seligman, a pioneer of positive psychology, happiness has three dimensions that can be cultivated: the Pleasant Life, the Good Life, and the Meaningful Life.

The Pleasant Life is realized if we learn to savor and appreciate such basic pleasures as companionship, the natural environment, and our bodily needs. The Good Life is achieved through discovering our unique virtues and strengths, and employing them creatively to enhance our lives. Lastly, there is the Meaningful Life, in which we find a deep sense of fulfillment by employing our unique strengths for a purpose that is greater than we are, or our highest hopes and dreams.

It is important to experience all three dimensions in order to create a mood that fosters joy, good spirits and well-being.

We have to be in a very clear and conscious state to navigate through the three dimensions of happiness effectively and maintain the happiness required to keep our balance. We also have to understand the lack of balance in our lives affects others; and when it does, we are responsible for their pain or discomfort.

For example, an alcoholic will rationalize that by drinking, he is only harming himself, but he doesn't realize how much pain other people feel due to his actions. He also fails to realize what he will lose by harming himself and others.

Achieving each of the three dimensions of happiness in some way should be our objective as each of them is important in living a fulfilled and purposeful life.

Playing the part

In 1998, I decided to try out for the role of "husband," and to my surprise, I got the part. I had been studying my lines ever since I ran into Tiffany during Florida A&M University's homecoming the year before. We knew each other in school but never really socialized.

I had no intention of going to homecoming; neither did she. We both just so happened to make a last-minute decision to attend. While there I went to an Alpha party with fraternity brothers, and there she was. She had on a black dress with a black and wife scarf. All I can recall is thinking to myself, "Is that Tiffany?"

Corporate America definitely looked good on her. I said hello and made small talk and after a few minutes went on my way. Later that evening we reconnected at another event. This time we talked at length. At its conclusion, I gave her my numbers (all five of them) and suggested that we stay in touch.

Months later she gave me a call unexpectedly. Tiffany has vivid dreams and said that she dreamed that something had happened to me and wanted to make sure I was ok. That conversation led to many others, and ultimately I fell in love and asked her to marry me. She said yes.

Now, although I won the role, I was not truly prepared to play it. When we got engaged, Tiffany and I moved in together and were going through a major transition. We had just relocated to Atlanta and were preparing for a wedding, building a new home and working new jobs.

Although Tiffany appeared all together, I felt like I was failing at everything, as if I had bitten off more than I could chew. Feeling overwhelmed, I began shutting down. My solution was to just not do anything.

I became a shell of my former self. I was basically going through the motions and didn't want to talk with anyone about anything.

Although I had reservations about how things were playing out, I didn't share. I wouldn't talk about my feelings because that wasn't who I had been. Instead, I tried to please her by giving her the Nick I thought she wanted or needed to see, but that wasn't sustainable because it wasn't me — yeah, it was far from my true self.

I knew I needed to get myself on course, but didn't know where to even begin. This was eating away at my relationship. I presented myself one way, and now I was allowing the pressure to expose something else that was obviously buried inside of me. My fiancé was glimpsing a side of the real me she had never seen.

This is an example of how messed up things can get when we attempt to please everyone and be who we are not; because sooner than expected, it will be to our detriment. It can become impossible to get any support or assistance, because the person we are portraying seems not to need anything -- so no one is offering help. Being unhappy can cause us to make poor decisions, affect our health, test our faith, and can ruin relationships. When we're not happy, we never reach our full potential and/or purpose; we're unable to receive blessings from or be a blessing to others, and our sadness can even shorten our life.

I'm not sure about you, but I don't want any of these issues plaguing my existence. Yes, it's true a positive attitude can change our environment. For those who are in leadership, it is especially important because every decision we make, large or small, affects at least three or more individuals. Making poor decisions under the influence of our unhappiness leaves casualties in the wake. Our unhappiness can make it hard for anyone around us to be happy.

The choice is yours

Repeat after me, "Many of the challenges or obstacles I face arise because of me." They are there for our good. As noted in Channel 1, these things make us stronger, wiser, and more valuable.

Now that we've gotten that out of the way, we can focus on not eliminating the challenges (because they are a part of life) but on making them manageable once we're tuned in and begin to understand them better.

I learned that if I wanted to be happy, I had to successfully manage my expectations and understand what I was asking for. I must avoid being general when I need to be specific. I must be confident in my "ask" and understand the importance of knowing when to ask with expectation.

You may need some tools to flip the happiness switch. Something as small as remembering to laugh daily can change your outlook and mood. Although you may have to force it at first, eventually it will become natural and change your mood. A key component to succeeding is to recognize how you feel at any given moment as you practice being present.

If you feel numb, like you are unable to give or receive love, you could be focusing on your weaknesses and not your strengths. This means it's time to consciously recalibrate yourself. To consciously recalibrate, you have to adjust your outlook on life. This allows you to put things in perspective to ensure that your mindset motivates and excites you.

Experience has taught me that it's up to me to correct that voice inside my head that has led me to think about the problems in my world and not look at the good in the world around me. It's not about seeking temporary gratification through overindulgence of things like food, drugs and alcohol, sex, television and social media. It's about creating things that help me sustain my happiness to find the balance I want and need.

I used to hear it often but didn't really subscribe to the belief that happiness is a choice, until I tried it. Today, I choose to be happy. Does that mean I'm always walking around with a huge smile and nothing ever bothers me? No. What it does mean is that I understand happiness is a choice, and that I can disallow what's going on around me to steal my joy.

When I have a spirit of gratitude, meaning that when I decide to shift my perspective and see the good in every situation, things begin to change. I don't have to allow my circumstance to define my mood. Yes, this is easier said than done; but as I've practiced it, my world has changed because my perspective changes. I begin to focus on my blessings rather than my burdens. I may not have everything I want, exactly how I want it, but my needs are being met and satisfied.

Who am I?

You'll never be happy until you're satisfied with the skin you're in and begin walking in the purpose you were designed to embrace. To do this, you must determine "who you are" before you can understand what you were born to achieve. Understanding who you are requires that you be real with yourself and determine what lane in life you are meant to travel, and then stay in it. Now let me say this: It's okay to change lanes as long as you first make a signal; but changing too often is a sign you don't know where you're going. Once you get off track, you lose time, and you often have a difficult time finding your way back. This can cause you to develop feelings of unhappiness. The secret of my success is to begin and then finish what I start.

Why am I unhappy?

In business, we start toward solutions by identifying the root cause or causes of an issue. To determine the root cause of the unhappiness in our life, we have to be real with ourselves.

Something that I do, which has helped me to improve my life, is to listen to the feedback that I get from other people, especially those people that are the closest to me. For example, there was a time when I was quick to dismiss Tiffany's ideas. She would give me advice on how to dress, talk, drive, etc., and I wouldn't listen. The reality is that she knows me like the back of my hands; and when I dismissed her point of view, it was because I was mad that she figured me out.

What can I do differently?

Are you dealing with grief, anger, resentment, and disappointment? If you said "yes," you're not alone. The majority of the population is dealing with the same things. I used to think I was unique in that manner, but I realized I'm not that special. We all have problems and we all suffer from unhappiness from time to time.

If focusing on how to be happy is difficult, you may need to reduce your number of responsibilities by shutting some things down and getting some rest. We often find ourselves overcommitting and carrying too much burden as a result of expectations. Sometimes you just have to let go, put yourself first, and then give yourself permission to stop in order to successfully manage your happiness.

A key to doing this is making sure you step up your prayer life. If you're only praying when you want something, change that channel; God wants more. If you are saying, "Well, I pray enough," make sure you're building a relationship with God and talking to Him like He's your best friend. You will be amazed how that one thing can help manage your happiness.

It took me a minute to realize that God is my ultimate counsel as well as the supplier of joy in my life; but it's necessary for me to identify wise counsel here on earth for understanding, too. You can't figure it out on your own nor should you try.

If you are breathing right now, guess what? You have issues. If you think you don't have any issues, you are lying to yourself, which may be your biggest issue. In order to solve your issues, you must be real with yourself. Unhappiness leads to addiction, poor decisions, adultery, divorce, and the list goes on. As we begin to seek things to fill the void, we often turn to unhealthy options.

Sometimes we have to pay attention to the people close to us and truly hear what they are saying. Another's unhappiness was my wake-up call, something we all need from time to time. There are times when your norm must be disturbed to propel you to do what's necessary to be happy. We usually know we need to change, but we don't do anything about it. The majority of times, it's the "fear to face it," but fear will cripple you.

Listening to people who are close to you is critical and can help you overcome the fear. Don't be too quick to dismiss that family member, friend or your spouse. If you dismiss loved ones, it's often because they see the true you and you are upset that they figured you out.

A prime example was my drinking. For years, Tiffany expressed concern with my drinking. I had picked up the alcohol habit in my formative years. In fact, anyone who knew "Big Nick" back then knew that's just what I did.

I didn't see anything wrong with it, but she saw it differently; she saw it as a problem. It hit me that if I didn't make a change, one day I might get too drunk and say something that could upset her or even worse, make her quit the marriage.

Not wanting that scenario to become my reality, I knew I had to change. Once I did let go of that habit, I realized the fog that I had been operating in. I had become a victim of the struggle rather than a victor over it.

As we work hard to manage our personal lives, professional lives and ourselves, our happiness is the cornerstone on which we should build every aspect of it.

Getting connected

To get started making the change, you must ask yourself, "What will bring me happiness and strengthen my connection to God?" If you have a connection to God, you understand what love is. You understand that He is your protection, provider, and source of your happiness. You also understand that fear is of the devil.

Once I got connected to God, I automatically let go of fear and now understand how to conduct myself, from my morality to my money, including the need to tithe by giving the 10 percent God requires of us.

Attitude adjustment (manna moments)

If happiness is what I want, I must ask for it. Through countless mistakes and engaging in the wrong activities, looking for the all-elusive happiness, I've learned the only person who can keep me from being happy is me. So, I've learned to ask God to provide and to accept "yes" as an answer; and now I know this: The things that create happiness are all within my reach.

My mentor and pastor, the late Bishop W. Ron Sailor Sr., always told me, "Nick, you have not because you ask not. Anything in this world you want, you have to ask for it."

I've learned to ask for peace and not allow my situation to dictate my attitude, which isn't always the easiest thing to do. Peace is truly what you seek. I've experienced money issues in the past and I've still been at peace. Money issues don't faze me because when I put it in perspective, I realize that it's all just "stuff." The true value is in the things that I can't replace. As long as I have my family, my health, and I'm in my right mind, that's really all I need.

I've also had to prioritize to make sure I was placing value on the things that were actually valuable. I stopped chasing money. If I lose it, I can always find more. I believe this because I know that God promised "manna for the day," but sometimes we complain as the Israelites did. "We get this manna every single day, it's nasty, and we wish we had something else," they murmured. The Israelites complained to Moses daily about the manna even though it was this same manna that was sustaining them through their journey to God's promise land. It's the same in our lives: God provides for us, but it's often not what we envision "manna" to look like.

"Look at this car, it's raggedy." But that car got you from point A to point B consistently. You made it to work on time...manna!

"My spouse gets on my last nerve." But your spouse's actions show you love. Your spouse saw past your flaws to marry you...manna!

"I can't stand this job; they don't appreciate me." But right now, that job is paying the bills and allowing you to take care of your family...manna, that's what it is!

If you recognize God's "manna moments" in your life, you will gain appreciation for His enduring love. That appreciation leads to fulfillment, which ultimately leads to happiness. With happiness, you can build a life of real peace. Happiness is often a matter of perspective; however, you may need to shift your views just a tad to get a fresh outlook and see the potential.

In case of emergency

I fly often for business and each time I travel, I'm always reminded of a proper life perspective. Every time I board a plane, before we take off, the flight attendant announces during the safety briefing those famous words, saying, "In case of emergency and there is a loss in cabin pressure, yellow oxygen masks will deploy from the ceiling compartment located above you ... Please make sure to secure your own mask before assisting others." This means put the oxygen mask on yourself and then help the person you're responsible for who is with you.

Sometimes you have to be unapologetically selfish in order to help yourself and others. If something is not making you happy, sometimes you have to say, "I choose me first" and there's nothing wrong with that.

If you don't choose you first, you will eventually have a resentful spirit. You'll be frustrated and end up with a negative attitude; and no matter how much you try to cover it up, it will always show in your expression, your disposition, and your spirit. You must focus on getting you — your very self or person — right first before you can really be any good to anyone else.

Seek and ye shall find

A few months back, an associate confided in me he was having issues with his marriage. He said he was unhappy and that he and his wife had grown apart. I asked him a simple question, which I now challenge you to think about: "What is it that you are seeking?"

What I've learned in life is that I always have to have a goal, something that I am working on or looking forward to reaching. This concept of goal setting is especially important in marriage. Some of the very best times I have with Tiffany are when we are working together toward a specific goal.

There's no better example of this than when we found out we were pregnant. We had decided to wait several years before having a child and now that it was imminent, we where in full gear. We spent weekends purchasing items, planning for Quinn's room, and we attended birthing classes and doctor's appointments. Some of the very best times we had during her pregnancy were in the evenings. One of the many items we had purchased was a machine that Tiffany wore around her belly each night for 30 minutes. This machine made the most aggravating sounds; however, it supposedly helped to stimulate brain activity and claimed to make babies more intelligent. Now, whether or not this is true I have no idea. What I do know is that I looked forward to that time each night as it became our time to bond, dream, or at the very least, complain about how awful a noise that contraption made.

According to Jaak Panskepp, a respected neuroscientist, of the seven core instincts in the human brain (anger, fear, panic, grief, maternal care, pleasure/play, and seeking), seeking is the most important. Achieving a milestone can be a great accomplishment. However, to maintain happiness, we will always need to continue to grow and continue to set goals for ourselves.

STAY TUNED TAKEAWAYS

- Recognize that happiness is a choice.

- Making someone happy is impossible if you aren't happy with yourself.

- Be unapologetically selfish when it comes to your personal happiness.

- Finding happiness may require you to make some vital changes to your perspectives about life and what's most important.

- Maintaining happiness requires you to want something more, and then seek until you find it.

Channel Three

WHERE THERE IS A WILL, THERE IS YOUR WHY

Willpower to purpose

A favorite phrase of my late grandmother, Mildred Nelson-Hayes, was "Grandson, just keep on living."

She meant we're going to have experiences in life that will test us and make us feel like we can't go on. Ultimately, to break through, you have to will yourself through.

Will is your "willpower," which can be the catalyst to establishing good habitual behavior that eventually takes over and steers your life. At the end of willing yourself through, if you pay attention to the signs and stay tuned, typically your "why" is nearby.

Finding your why — your motivation — requires you to think introspectively and ask yourself, "Why am I doing what I'm doing?"

Your answer to this question will help you discover your motivation for your current path or maybe the one you are yet to embrace.

Life is best lived on purpose. Life is not about our titles, our daily responsibilities, or even our short- and long-term goals. All those things can and will change. Finding your "why," your purpose, means identifying the real reason you are here, the very reason you exist.

When your thoughts are filled with heart-wrenching questions like: "Why did that horrible thing happen to me? Why do good things happen to bad people? Why do bad things happen to good people? I'm doing it the right way, but I lost my job, and my children are going crazy," often God has a lesson that He wants you to learn. Or maybe He wants someone else to learn through your living. Maybe God needed your life to be a testament to another person going through something similar, someone who needed to see what overcoming looks like.

As I sit back and analyze my life, I realize I have been "willing" after the wrong stuff for a long time, and I'd venture to say I'm not alone. Working as an executive in such a fast-paced and high-stress industry as entertainment marketing, I was always chasing after the next deal. Not to say that I shouldn't, as selling is a part of the job; but I should not have let it become an all-consuming thing. Selling ideas is my job; however, selling ideas is not my purpose. We should not allow our professional life to overshadow our home life or to be seen as our purpose.

My will is strong because of my why, which is my purpose. My purpose is bigger than I am; and at times, that can be intimidating. I, too, often ask myself why certain things are happening in my life and why it is so challenging to get my footing just right. But in these moments, I recall the scripture that says, "There will be times of trouble." Therefore, I can't be thrown off balance by the challenges I encounter in my life, because it is already written.

If I stop every time things get a little hard, I would never progress. I've learned to use trouble as my power to fuel my movement when I feel empty. I know I was created for more than just "getting by," flying under the radar, or hiding in the back of the class.

Our "why" should motivate us and give us a reason to stay tuned. When we ask ourselves why we have a desire to realize a dream, help others, earn a substantial income, be a success in our industry, build a successful business, and/or enter a marriage or partnership, we get closer to the root of "why" God placed us here in the first place.

Uncovering these important components to finding peace is critical to success. Recently, the American Psychological Association's annual Stress in America Survey showed that participants regularly cited lack of willpower as the No. 1 reason for not following through with changes. Knowing your "why" and having willpower are essential pieces to solving life's puzzle; and when revealed, they help to motivate and propel you closer to achieving your purpose.

The power of the will and the why

To find the power that propelled me, I began with prayer. I talked with God to ask for strength and guidance. I also talked to others to get wise counsel. I learned that self-determination was instrumental in this process. I had to be my own cheerleader and be able to motivate myself. I learned that I couldn't depend on someone else to "will" me through; instead, I had to speak to myself and believe that I had the ability to move mountains when it appeared that they were too high to get over.

I had to accept the fact that bad things will happen, and I'm okay with it. During one of our many personal conversations, my pastor taught me that in life there are four inevitabilities, meaning we should not ask "will" they happen but "when" they will happen. These four inevitable events are what I call, "the 4Ds of Life: Death, Disease, Disappointment and Disaster," and they are unavoidable components of living. They are the flip side of the coin of positive happenings.

The 4Ds of Life are feelings and events that we all will experience. Remember, God said, "There will be times of trouble," so it's now your responsibility to trust Him, praise your way through, and figure out what you have to do to deal with them.

Experiencing one of the Ds of life can cause you to feel like you are drained emotionally and want to give up; but experiencing multiple Ds at once can paralyze you and make you feel as if you can't move on.

In 2013, I was slapped hard with a few of the Ds in a very short window. Business issues, along with my father's death and my pastor's death in the same year, knocked the breath out of me. As if that were not enough, life hit me with my mom's health decline, as she began to slip further into dementia. These experiences had the power to stop me, but I was able to dig deep down to uncover my will to keep going in the midst of it all.

This is when I thought, not only is there merit in the saying "Where there's a will, there's a way," but understanding comes from a variation that tells me, "Where there's a will, there's a why."

Once I discovered my purpose and clearly defined "why," I was able to sustain my drive. Discovering and tapping into my "why" showed me it was my job to identify what was important to me, what gave me peace, what excited me, and what pushed me forward.

I had to come out of hiding. Being in hiding was so unlike me. In the past, I was hard to miss. See, I used to be a heavy guy, thus the nickname "Big Nick." I went through my Luther Vandross phase, with my weight up one day and down the next. It was like being on a cruel roller coaster that just wouldn't end. It was after I watched my father's health deteriorate as a result of not taking care of himself that I began to change.

I was tired of feeling trapped. I wanted to be there for my family and be able to spend time with the grandchildren I hoped to have one day. And I didn't just want to look at them from a distance and be unable to interact and engage in conversation, all because I chose not to take care of myself. I watched my father deteriorate from a globetrotter to a man trapped inside of his own body. He was diagnosed with diabetes at 38, but for years after that, he didn't eat right or do other things he was supposed to do, like exercising his body and regulating his intake of sugar.

My pops was a smart man but very hardheaded. He wanted to live his life how he wanted to live it. This became a never-ending challenge, because once you get sick and you don't address it, things just compile and expand.

Tough decisions

My father was a PhD professor in the Political Science Department and Chair of the African-American Studies Department at The Ohio State University. In my mind — and in the minds of people I knew — he was "The Man." I watched him wear sharp suits to work daily.

He was the first person I knew that had a brand. He was recognized as one of the pioneers for the establishment of the discipline of African American and African studies in the United States and was instrumental in the creation of The Ohio State University's Department of African American Studies. He was one of the leading producers of African American PhDs and was just different, smart, outspoken, unafraid, and clean as the board of health.

It was hard seeing him go through his health challenges, one after another. It's like dealing with an old car when things start to breakdown and you can't do anything about it other than knowing that it's on its way out. The truth is you can look for a new car but you can't look for a new body.

One evening while at home with my family, I got an unwanted call that I knew in my spirit inevitably one day I would receive: My dad was in a hospital in Columbus, Ohio, had taken a turn for the worse and had been moved to intensive care. It wasn't looking good, as he was breathing through a ventilator; but I was remaining optimistic and prayerful.

A few days later, again while at home, I received a call. This time my dad's brother, sister and my grandmother were on the other line. It was an intervention.

"Baby, this is your grandmother. I think it's time that you let your daddy go."

This was one of the hardest things I had ever heard, let alone contemplated. I was devastated by her comment. Even though my heart knew it, I still wasn't ready to let go. I decided to go back to Ohio with my wife to check on him and make a decision.

As soon as I walked in the door, tears filled my eyes when he looked at me. Although he had been unconscious, for that moment he was fully aware. I knew he could see the hurt in my eyes and responded by shaking his head and through his tube softly whispering, "Aww man." He knew the decision he required me to make.

My pops was a brilliant man who could have gone much further, but I watched him give up. I knew he gave up because he felt trapped. Diabetes and kidney disease had taken a hold of his health and had taken away his quality of life. Lying helpless on a ventilator wasn't his brand. This wasn't the life he had worked to create.

During this moment I needed advice. I needed my wife. Tiffany gently grabbed my hand and we sat down on the bench together and reviewed the options. She asked me tough questions that made me think rationally. That helped me to look beyond the emotions of the moment but think about what was best not for me but for my father.

After a long talk with God, and Tiffany's help in going over the options, I did decide that it was time to take Dad off the machine. I called the family, informed them of my decision, and a few days later, we were all by his bedside. Friends, family, loved ones were all there to say our farewells, and my father made a beautiful transition from life to death, surrounded by what truly mattered: his family.

None of his degrees mattered at that moment, none of the accolades nor the promotions, and definitely not the money. What mattered was his family by his side. He was surrounded by love, which was the harvest from the seeds he had planted all of his life. My only pain was that he had regrets on time lost with us because of the demands of his career.

After Dad passed, I was hurt and quite frankly pissed off for a while because I didn't want to be the one to make that decision. Who wants to be the one that says enough is enough for your old man's life? But I began to see that it was all a part of the journey I had to take.

That was the 'D' that almost wiped me out. Looking at my father fade and lose his battle with the 'D' of disease made me fully understand that I have to enjoy what I have right now, because tomorrow isn't promised.

The power of now

It's not something we like to think about, but we're all just one moment away from one of the 4 Ds of Life drastically changing our lives. I do not intend to depress you, but rather to impress upon you the power of now. I'm a realist and understand this because I've experienced it and watched others close to me experience it. I've seen what happens, as you grow older and your circle of friends gets smaller, as they pass away. As your community gets smaller, life can get lonely and all you have to hold on to are the memories. If you haven't balanced well, you will find yourself alone with memories of all the things your profession afforded you financially, rather than the priceless memories of spending time with your family.

I was compelled to examine my health and myself because my father didn't get a chance to enjoy his retirement. He didn't get a chance to spend time with his grandson. He didn't get a chance to spend more time with his wife, partially because he wasn't tuned in. He got caught up in the trap that catches many of us, chasing something that has no real substance while neglecting something that can't be replaced. He didn't take time to pay attention to his health and therefore he paid the ultimate price. I often think if only he had seen the importance of tuning in, maybe he would still be here to do the things he envisioned himself doing. On the other hand, on a spiritual level, perhaps he "chose" to be an example for me, thus serving as the catalyst to influence me to turn my life around.

From plight to purpose

I had to speak to myself and say, "Nick, you need to get your life together."

I am in my forties and I've only been diagnosed with hypertension, so I take my medication and watch what I eat. I remind myself to get up, move and exercise. I'm not a part of that percentage of people that can just eat what they want and not gain weight. Remember, I was Luther Vandross.

We all go through stuff, but many of us don't always get that lesson. I chose to learn from my experiences, and I had to ask myself, "Why did I go through what I went through with my old man?"

I believe that purpose is directly correlated to the challenges that we've had in our lives. I've seen guys say, "You know what? I never had a father." Therefore, they "will" themselves to be the very best father they can be.

I thank God for the blessing to be present at this very moment in time. Some may say, "I really don't like my job and I don't like my circumstance." If this sounds like you, this is when you have to "will" yourself through it with a good attitude and learn a new skill set. Until you figure that out, you're not where you're supposed to be. You must go through the obstacles and stay "in tune" so you can recognize and hold on to that intrinsic purpose in your circumstances. Otherwise, you'll miss it.

People often ask how I've been able to succeed in my pursuits, but it's simple: the support of my family and refusing to quit. Quitting is not a part of my brand. I've learned to persevere in the midst of challenges. I have learned that my family is my "why." I get a chance to afford my family a specific lifestyle because I'm the provider. But I also need to be present.

When you're in business, especially as an entrepreneur, your work can consume your life. We often say we're working hard for our family, but without balance, you might not be doing them any favors. How is your job truly affecting your family? Are you always on your phone, not spending time with them, being on vacation but not allowing yourself to be truly present? Is this the way you are working for your family?

In reality, you could be working so hard because it's what you want to do. What your kids want is for you to be a dad, and your spouse wants a helpmeet. They all want someone who is going to listen, spend quality time, provide some counsel and sometimes just a shoulder to lean on or a lap to lie on; but you can't be that if you aren't present. Sure, they may like what the job provides financially or in prestige, but in reality, they care more about being with YOU.

This all may sound a little daunting — finding balance yet living your purpose and being present all the while is crucial. Let me review three necessary components for achieving your objective of finding peace and balance:

- First, you must tap into your "why" to establish the motivation for change and set a clear goal.

- Second, you need to monitor your behavior toward that goal.

- Third, you should tap into your hunger to succeed, which I call your willpower.

Whether your goal is to lose weight, spend more time with your family, study more, or spend less time wasting time, willpower is a critical step to achieving that outcome.

Could your purpose be tied to your fears? I've found that the things I'm afraid of actually help move me closer to my purpose. Think about it. In the Bible, Moses questioned God, asking Him, "Why would they listen to me? I'm slow to speak."

He was afraid to use his voice because of the imperfections in his speech, but the one thing he feared was the one thing God used to do a perfect work. You must believe in something greater than you, beyond the "all about me" attitude, and be patient on the course as you work it out. I haven't always been a man of faith; but over time, my faith has matured as I have learned that my purpose is to praise God with my worship, proclaiming His greatness and being a light that will draw others closer to Him.

The question I have to ask myself daily is, "How do I do that today?" I learned over time that faith without works is dead. This means you must believe, but you also must follow up that belief with a dose of action, consistently. I want to live my very best life right now so I will build a multitude of beautiful memories over the years (my health and God's will giving me a long life). And I'm content with that.

STAY TUNED TAKEAWAYS

- A strong why creates an achievable how.

- Stop focusing on those things that don't have substance and neglecting the things that can't be replaced.

- Get out of your own way. Your purpose is bigger than you are.

- You do have to face the 4Ds of Life (Death, Disease, Disappointment, and Disaster); you don't have to let them consume you.

- Be your own cheerleader. Don't give in to a "woe is me" way of thinking or even worse, depression. Will yourself out of it and move on.

Channel Four

CHUTES AND LADDERS

Major changes

One of my favorite childhood board games was Chutes and Ladders, created by Milton Bradley. The game consists of a square board made up of 100 squares (10 by 10 squares). Players spin a spinner to determine how many squares to move their game piece, called a "pawn." If their final spot rests at the bottom of a ladder, they get to go up; and if it rests at the top of a chute, they must go down. Players want to land at the base of a ladder so they can race ahead of the other players with the goal of reaching the 100th square at the end of the board.

The "ups and downs" of the game represent moral choices and their consequences, good deeds being "ladders" and bad deeds being "chutes."

Whenever I think about my professional journey, this game is the simplest way I know to sum it up. In the spirit of the game, I have spun the wheel regarding my career on many occasions hoping that I would land at the top of the ladder. In some instances I have been successful; others, not so much. To me, the thrill is still in playing the game, knowing that if I do slide down, I have a chance to make it right back to the top again.

Now the key to any game is to understand its rules of engagement. As it relates to my career, I learned the rules to the game while attending FAMU. There is something remarkable about the lessons students learn at a black college. One thing I learned in particular is what I did not want to do professionally.

Throughout my entire life, especially in high school, I had an affinity for music. I loved to write and produce songs, and I played the keyboards, drums, and bass. I was a part of my high school choir, produced a rap group, and even opened up for the then-rapper, Ice Cube during his Columbus, Ohio, stop on his very first solo tour. When it came time for me to decide on a major, it only made sense that I pursue music; not so much because I had a firm interest in it, but because I thought it would be easy.

My introduction to the FAMU School of Music occurred before the start of my freshman year when I was invited to participate in the Marching 100 band camp that summer. In truth, I only did it for my father, who was a former band member at his alma mater, the University of Arkansas Pine Bluff.

It was on those clay fields during those hot sunny days in Tallahassee that my love and affinity for music began to wane. I would see so many beautiful young ladies on the yard and can remember them looking at me like, "You smell!" This discomfort about my decision to be in the marching band stayed with me throughout the summer. At the conclusion of band camp, I invited my father to see me in my one and only marching band performance. After my performance he asked if I planned to participate during the school year, and I told him I had a conflict due to my vocal music courses. This was a lie, but it worked for me.

In the fall of 1991, I began my coursework in the School of Music and quickly learned that it was not as easy as I thought it would be. This was primarily because I could not read music, though I could play instruments. This immediately put me at a disadvantage and required me to work harder than I could imagine. At that point in my life, hard work was something I was not interested in doing. I wanted to have a good time and enjoy my newfound independence.

I managed to make it through my first year with decent grades but with less than a positive attitude. During the summer of 1992, I went back to Columbus to work. That summer, the movie Boomerang came out, starring Eddie Murphy. This film and its iconic character Marcus Graham would forever change my life. I discovered that there were other outlets I could use to be creative and make lots of money — more specifically, advertising.

As I watched the story unfold, I was completely taken by the character Murphy portrayed. I wanted to be Marcus Graham. I wanted to do something creative in advertising, but I didn't know where to even start, especially since there was no advertising program at FAMU.

In the fall of 1992, I went back to school determined to change majors. The School of Business and Industry (SBI) had a marketing program; however, since it was one of the best schools in the country, it was extremely competitive to get in, and I simply did not have the grades. I recall becoming increasingly frustrated because I knew I wanted to change directions and didn't know how to go about it.

Every day, I would see the brothers in SBI in their suits walking up and down the yard with confidence because they knew they were preparing to enter into a world of business, power and money. On the other hand, all I could think about was that I was headed for poverty as a music teacher in a school in some small town.

Frustrated, I called my dad one afternoon and told him that I did not like the path I was going down. I remember him, in all of his wisdom, saying, "Son, you know how to talk your way in and out of anything. Have you ever thought about going into public relations?"

At the time, I had no idea what public relations or being a publicist really meant, but once my father said it, I was intrigued. After investigating the program, I decided to change majors. I exited the School of Music and entered the School of Journalism to pursue a major in public relations with a minor in business.

As I became more familiar with public relations, I coincidentally learned about advertising. The more I learned, the more I discovered that I was actually good at it. However, to be great, and more specifically to get a job, I knew I needed some real world experience. The summer after my sophomore year, one afternoon, I began looking through the Yellow Pages on a whim for agencies that would give me an opportunity to learn.

Cade & Associates Advertising, Inc., a full-service advertising agency and integrated marketing communications firm located in Tallahassee, was the second number I called. The person on the other end of the line said the firm didn't offer an internship program but if I showed up, they would find work for me to do, provided I did not mind working without any wages.

That afternoon, I went to the agency and became its very first intern. My job description at Cade consisted of running errands, assisting with administrative items, and developing creative ideas. During the summer, I developed a close bond with the owners of the company and was soon offered a paid position, which I happily accepted. I went on to work for Cade for the remainder of my time at FAMU through graduation.

Up and down like Wall Street

Instead of entering the workforce right after graduation from FAMU, I decided to increase my knowledge of advertising; and at the suggestion of my father, I applied and was accepted into The Ohio State University. This is where the rubber would meet the road. I was Dr. Nelson's son. I couldn't fail or I would tarnish the great reputation my father had built. This is when the grind began.

My strategy was simple. I would study, take my education seriously, and take myself seriously. The real world was around the corner, and I had to sustain myself because I liked being independent.

While in graduate school, I interned with Satchi and Satchi, a global communications and advertising agency network with 140 offices in 76 countries. This continued to fuel my passion for creativity as I learned the game. I had rolled the dice and was on the rise.

As I approached graduation, I began attending job interviews for various opportunities with advertising agencies in Columbus and across the country. I received offers from several agencies; however, the average offer was roughly $15,000-$20,000 per year. That was not quite what I had in mind and would definitely not accommodate my lifestyle. The feeling I had in 1991 of sliding down the board began to creep in again as I raced against the clock trying to prepare for my next move.

Fortunately, I did not stay down for long. I started my ascent again soon when I accepted a job with Andersen Consulting, now Accenture, one of the world's largest IT consulting and services firms. At first, I was reluctant to take it, because I knew nothing about technology but knew I needed something at least to fuel my passion. Prior to accepting that position, I sought counsel from my father once again, as I knew he would provide great perspective on this most important decision. When I presented the offer to him and asked if I should consider it, he looked at me and asked,

"How much are they offering?"

"About $45,000," I replied, nonchalantly.

My dad didn't miss a beat and immediately said,

"Fool, take the job!"

The following week, I signed my commitment letter. My path was set. I was moving up the ladder again.

Coming out of grad school, I prided myself on my knowledge of advertising and marketing; but my confidence was shaken when I began to feel like a fish out of water not long after joining Andersen. A huge part of my role at Andersen was writing code, and it almost killed me. I can remember working on an assignment and feeling lost, as if I wasn't adding any value. I was making mistakes in my new role, and it felt miserable.

I wasn't a "sitting in front of your desk all day coding" type of guy, and it showed. I eventually was removed from my very first assignment and sent back to the office to look for my next consulting opportunity. In consulting terms, I was on "the bench."

Translation: I was in jeopardy of losing my job. Instead of pursuing what I loved, I had pursued the money, and I hated it. Down the chute I went.

After several project assignments, I began to learn different skills that did not require me to code and that allowed more interaction with clients. After obtaining my project management professional (PMP) certification, I found my way back up again.

I moved back to Columbus, Ohio, to take a job with a start-up by the name of Smart Talk Tele-services. Eight months later, I was laid off and started my way down again. At that point, I was engaged, about to get married, so Tiffany and I decided to make the move to Atlanta for a fresh start. I was on my way back up the ladder when I got a job at Alltel Information Services in Alpharetta, Georgia, in the project management office.

From there, I spun the wheel and left for the chance to make more money as a project manager at another start-up called Syncor Technologies, a pharmaceutical company. A year later, I was laid off and began spiraling down the chute. I went back to Alltel Information Services, got hired again, and started my way back up. I eventually left there for a job at UPS, which was described as a "resume burner," which meant I could work there forever, and that was my trajectory as I could feel my ascent. Several years later, I left UPS after starting LIQUID SOUL. I had come full circle and ascended to the 100th square by establishing a career in marketing and advertising on my own terms. Game Over.

In all my ups and downs, the biggest thing I learned was that balance is nearly impossible when you are constantly in a state of transition. If it's not planted, it's impossible for it to grow, and this was the case for my career. You might have experienced something similar on your climb up the ladder before you slid back down, or maybe you've been able to maintain but still are unable to locate the oh-so-elusive balance.

You may even be stuck on the middle rungs of the ladder waiting for someone to save you. If that's what you are doing, I need you to know that no one is coming for you. It's either climb or jump, but either way, you have to make the decision. Choose wisely.

STAY TUNED TAKEAWAYS

- When deciding on a career, it's just as important to know what you don't want to do as what you want to do.

- Keep calm through life's ups and downs. When good things happen, thank God, and when bad things happen, thank God. In the end, it's all for your good.

- Balance is impossible if you are always in a state of transition. If you are not planted, it's impossible for you to grow.

- Don't chase after money; let money chase after you.

- In life, you will approach intersections or detours. If you don't know which way to go, seek counsel. If you get lost along the way, know it is okay to turn back around and start all over again. You will soon get it right. Don't quit!

Channel Five

A BRAND APART

A hard look in the mirror

R ecently I was asked by a colleague, "What is a personal brand and how can I develop mine?" She said she was asking because she had noticed enhancements in my image and professional reputation and wanted to achieve the same.

For those of you who may be unfamiliar with the term "personal branding," I will explain by starting with the basics and define what a brand is.

A brand is a product, service, or concept that is publicly distinguished from other products, services, or concepts so that it can be easily communicated, and is usually marketed.

Translation: A brand is a combination of those unique attributes that separate you from the crowd.

One example can be found with one of my favorite brands, the technology products company Apple. Apple made computers for two decades, and after rocky sales and low margins in the 1990s, the company was on the verge of bankruptcy in 1997. The shift came when Steve Jobs instilled a new corporate philosophy of recognizable products and simple design.

Today, Apple sells more than just computers. The company builds creative products that are well made and enhanced by beautiful packaging. These products easily connect with consumers by promoting a perceived value that solves problems and fills a need. It's not that no other companies are building good computers; it's just that Apple, through its advertising and unique product design, communicates a perceived value to consumers, which drives emotion and triggers a response — sales.

Similar to Apple, over the past several years, I have spent time developing and fine-tuning my personal brand. Defining and creating my personal brand has been an uncomfortable experience because it has required me to do some serious self-evaluation and tackle some issues head on. One of my biggest issues being my weight, I also had to address my style, conversation, personal and professional relationships, confidence level, belief systems, and my faith. Bottom line, I had to take a hard look in the mirror and figure out who I was, what I wanted to achieve, and how I wished to be perceived by others.

After much trial and error, I am pleased with my results. The person I am today is the best and most complete version of me to date. Like most computer programs, this latest version comes with various bug fixes and enhancements resulting from life experiences and user feedback.

There's only one

If you were to search for me across the Internet, you will find that there are many Nicholas Nelsons, and even more Nick Nelsons; however, there is only one Nick F. Nelson. Separating yourself from the pack is important and can be your professional fast-pass, thereby accelerating you down a certain lane.

Although I am Nick F. Nelson today, that hasn't always been the case. In my lifetime, I've had several name changes; some I developed on my own, others were handed down by individuals at various points along the way. I've been "Little Nicky" to family members throughout my childhood. And I've been "Dr. Nelson's son" to my father's colleagues and my friends, too.

For a while, I was "Nick Nice," a wannabe rapper/singer in my teenage years when I was a cross between a chubbier Al B. Sure! and the rapper Heavy D.

I became "Big Nick the Alpha" at Florida A&M University, whittled down to "Big Nick," a name that some call me to this day.

Once I started my professional and personal journey, I became "Nick Nelson" — the corporate professional. When I received my project management certification, I became "Nick Nelson, PMP." Those were particularly tough years from a branding perspective, because many people did not know that PMP stood for

Project Management Professional. When written out, and definitely, when I said it, the name sounded more like "PIMP," which made for some interesting conversations.

Tiffany refers to me affectionately as "Husband," and I must say that this version of me contained the most bugs of them all. You see, up until I got married, life was all about me. Growing up spoiled as an only child, I was accustomed to having my way and putting my needs first. I quickly learned that, in marriage, this line of thinking doesn't work. Tiffany continuously challenges me to be a better man and has helped to upgrade my way of thinking, acting and behaving.

After leaving corporate America and starting LIQUID SOUL with my college friend and business partner, Tirrell, I found myself often referenced to as "That LIQUID SOUL guy" due to the unique name of our company and the success we've had.

"Dad" is just about the best name I've ever had. There is little in life that brings me more joy than being a father. When my son was a little boy, and even to this day, I sometimes find myself just staring at him. I recall my own father used to do the same to me, and I would think, "What are you looking at"? I get it now. It's the pure amazement that I had the ability to help procreate someone so beautiful.

Lastly, there is "Deacon Nick." I remember the first time I visited Christ the King Baptist Church, where I've been a member now for over 15 years. I recall talking to Tiffany about how I just didn't feel comfortable interacting with "Church Folks." As fate and God would have it, years later, the man I would come to know as Bishop W. Ron Sailor Sr. asked me to become a deacon. I immediately thought, "You've got the wrong guy." He said that I could think about it, as long as I needed, but when I came back to him, my answer should be yes. Well, indeed it was yes, and I have given the Lord my YES ever since.

Your personal brand in 3D

When establishing my personal brand, I took a 3D approach. My 3D is not like the films you find in the theater but rather a methodology that consists of three phases: DEFINE your brand,

DEVELOP your brand mission statement and strategy, and DELIVER your brand identity and message. This proactivity begins with a mission statement, your brand perspective of your target market or audience, and your strategy as to how you want to do it.

Step One:
Define Your Brand

This stage requires serious soul searching and is truly the most important step. You must identify and have an inventory of all the things that make you who you are. This includes your skills, hobbies you enjoy, roles you play, the things in life that you value, what makes you happy, your fears and frustrations, the icon or role model you wish to emulate, your professional and personal goals, and your unique value proposition.

In this stage, you will seek to better understand your purpose, how you are perceived personally, professionally, and online, as well as what you would like to achieve in the short and long term. In essence, you're defining who you are.

Step Two:
Develop Your Brand Mission Statement and Strategy

You must develop your Brand Mission Statement, which is a tool used by businesses and individuals to help them define who they are and why they do what they do. This includes the value you create, plus who you're creating it for, and the expected outcome. Your brand strategy should be authentic to who you are and should take into consideration your brand values, target audience, brand promise, and your brand identity or personality.

Step Three:
Deliver Your Brand Identity and Message

This is the stage where the rubber hits the road and you transition from strategy to tactical executions across various online and offline communication channels. You must be able to deliver your brand identity and message to communicate effectively with your target. This can be accomplished through blogs, video content, social media, lunch-n-learns, and mentoring.

There are multiple ways to effectively communicate and connect with the people that you desire to reach. It may be networking events, coffee chats, social media, personal notes, and email, to name a few. In order to determine if you're being effective, you must listen to feedbacks and monitor the results, metrics, opinions, and the gravity of how others respond to your messages.

Getting noticed in a good way

Once you decide to brand yourself, it's important to not only know your lane, but also own it. To drive down that lane as hard as you can, make sure that the right people notice you and you're building as many relationships as possible along the way.

For example, as it relates to my company LIQUID SOUL, our lane is strategic communications for entertainment and consumer brands. Because many of our clients reside on the west coast, I travel back-and-forth from Atlanta to Los Angeles regularly. While in Los Angeles, my business partner and I may visit any number of film and television studio lots for meetings. Many times, we are the only black faces in the room. The mere fact that we are in the room should be impressive enough; however, it's not our presence in the room that matters, but rather the impact we make while there. It starts the moment we walk in the door.

We appear as two confident, well-dressed, well-spoken, insightful black men. That image not only gets us noticed, it gets us deals. The great thing is that it's not any sort of facade; it's genuinely who we are.

The goal should be the same for you: To be noticed in a good way, to have confidence in yourself and the services you provide. Competition will always be there, but you must understand what you do well. Determine if there are areas of improvement or if you need to work to differentiate yourself by offering a specialty that will make you stand out from the crowd.

The real deal

The world we live in today is very personality focused. So many people want to be influencers or desire to be experts but do not have sufficient knowledge or experience. They are just Googling their way through. On the surface, they may seem as if they have it all together; however, I would encourage you to stop looking with your eyes, since most times things are not as picture perfect as they appear.

Having thousands of friends or followers on social media does not mean you have real influence. Many times, it all translates into temporary entertainment. You see, people may love watching you make a fool out of yourself or love talking about you because it makes them feel a little bit better about themselves. You have to be certain the brand image you are putting out there is genuine and the best representation of who you are; because that's what people will remember, and at the end of the day, that's what's sustainable.

STAY TUNED TAKEAWAYS

- Differentiate yourself from others. Leverage personal branding as your fast-pass to accelerating your career.

- Don't be search-engine smart and experience stupid. You can't GOOGLE experience; you have to live experience. You can't GOOGLE mistakes; you have to make mistakes.

- Influence is not who follows you but what people do because of you.

- Don't focus on your flaws; focus on how you can overcome them.

- Take a 3D approach to personal branding by defining your brand, developing a strategy, and delivering on it.

Channel Six

BE CAREFUL HOW YOU TREAT PEOPLE

Treat 'em right

The thing about staying tuned is you are relishing the moment by being present. For a long time, I didn't relish or appreciate the moment — my now. I was there today and gone tomorrow. For example, to this day, I have roommates I haven't talked to since I graduated from college. Once I left, I never looked back. That's because I didn't place value on relationships, so I didn't foster or nurture them. They had no meaning.

Relationships can mean different things to different people. As we go through life, we will meet a variety of people and we will build relationships with them, whether they are good, bad, or downright unhealthy. The key is to treat people how you want to be treated.

At LIQUID SOUL, when it's time to have tough conversations with employees, we take them to the roof. It's actually a patio at the top of our building. We don't take them up there to toss them over, but rather to speak privately without fear of others overhearing. One employee I took to the roof was extremely unhappy to find out I was letting him go. The last thing he said to me before departing was, "You really need to be careful how you treat people."

I felt that we had treated him fairly, but that statement resonated within me. We do have to be careful how we treat people. This doesn't just go for employees, but people, in general. This must apply to anyone you meet on your climb because things have a way of coming back around, and you just may meet the same person or people on the way down. Relationships play an immensely important role in our lives. So it is more important than ever to build good, long lasting relationships by treating people right.

To increase our odds of successfully navigating relationships, we have to master the art of managing people as well as their expectations. We all have an inherent desire to be connected to others in some way, because we are highly evolved individuals. For us, "to love and to be loved" is a very basic necessity to life.

What sometimes makes the concept of relationships unattractive is the work required to sustain them, especially if it is not balanced. We get frustrated because we are burdened by carrying a load that we feel someone else should be carrying. The better approach is to be a good team player and avoid being selfish in the wrong way. Contrary to popular belief, it's okay to be selfish, but not selfish in a way that's negatively affecting or hurting someone else.

The Bible has various examples that show how relationships are God's gift to man. God never intended nor desires for man to be alone. What He desires, and also commands, is for us to love one another. Unfortunately, sometimes we are so obsessed with other things that we forget how essential love is. Relationships begin and end with how we treat each other.

The power of discernment

When you want to enter into a relationship, use discernment. If someone wants to be in a relationship with you, seek to understand why. For instance, I run a small agency; and for me, it's very important that anybody we hire have not only the right expertise but the right spirit. A person's skill sets can be improved, but the wrong spirits in your environment can destroy your business.

Good relationships are essential. Make sure you develop them with people you can trust, who you care about, and who care about you. This is what defines a good relationship. It's not about expecting something in return; it's about giving of yourself willingly, not resting on your laurels, and continuously working to improve it.

It's not all about you

When building real relationships, we shouldn't have our focus entirely centered on just the benefits we can get from them. Good relationships aren't based on that, but rather on an inward desire to love others regardless of who they are or what authority they have over you. Look for quality in any relationship. Depth and sincerity should be most important. I would rather have a few good, solid and rewarding relationships rather than focus on too many people who slip in and out of my life whenever they please.

I'm not a betting man, but if I were, I would guess you have some individuals in your personal network with whom you haven't connected in a while. I encourage you to take the time and reach out. Reestablishing relationships is the fastest path to generating new ones. As you are rebuilding those relationships, be sure to ask questions about things to do and places to go; and let them know what you are personally trying to achieve, and see if they can recommend any other resources. Lastly, while trying to diversify your network, invite your new friends or associates into your world; because at the end of the day, it is about sharing experiences and learning to appreciate what each person brings to the table.

Now comes the hard part — maintaining relationships. Staying connected is difficult enough with our closest friends. Now, making the time to sustain and grow relationships with individuals from different backgrounds makes this task feel much more daunting. This is where an understanding of your professional and personal objectives comes into play. You must have some filter to prioritize the right way. Once you have your list solidified, understand that it will constantly change.

Stay in touch through a combination of "high touch" and "low touch" tactics. "High touch" tactics include coffee chats, lunch/dinner, or office visits. "Low touch" tactics include responding to social media posts, initiating a quick telephone call, or sending an email just to say hello. It all helps to build relationships and keeps us connected to others so they may be a blessing to us and so we may be the same.

Leaders must lead

One of the sayings my bishop frequently repeated to me and my deacon brothers was, "Leaders must lead." He was teaching us that if we were to be seen as leaders in the church, we had to act as leaders.

As a small business owner, my employees look to me for advice on any number of personal and professional issues. Other than client meetings, I spend a tremendous amount of time daily teaching and guiding. In my business, my people are my assets, as I am not selling products or widgets. Therefore, they represent me. Once I made the decision to transition professionally from 'doer' to 'manager,' then to 'owner,' I immediately took on the responsibility of leading people; and, therefore, if I want my business to flourish, I must be in a healthy relationship with them, which is driven by mutual respect and the desire to achieve more through collective efforts.

Leaders help themselves and others to do the right things. They set direction, build an inspiring vision, and create something new. Leadership is about mapping out where you need to go to "win" as a team or an organization; and it is dynamic, exciting and inspiring. Yet, while leaders set the direction, they must also use management skills to guide their people to the right destination, in a smooth and efficient way.

Leadership will make or break your company. Research shows that in most cases, employees quit managers, not companies per se.

Leadership is not for everyone, nor is everyone capable of leading. One of the biggest realities of leadership is that it's lonely. There are tons of expectations and you rarely get congratulated or even told "thank you," for that matter. But if you can get over those hurdles and still have the desire to push ahead, you know you're destined to lead.

I describe my leadership style of management as management by walking around. I can learn just about everything I need to know by asking one question using three simple words "How's it going?"

To determine the pulse of my employees and clients, I ask this question each day. I've learned to stay tuned in to my business affairs, and the amount of information I garner from those three words is often incredible. I learn about what's going on in my staff's worlds, what's happening in their personal lives, and what opportunities they have for growth. By not just acting concerned, but actually being concerned, you build a connection. That connection builds a bond that motivates others to have your best interest at heart. It's simple: You must care or they won't.

Much of my leadership style came from trial and error. I've developed my own technique by taking pieces of proven and effective styles I learned along the way. I have had leaders who were unbearable, making unreasonable demands constantly. I've also had leaders who were too lenient and watched how their employees ran all over them. Observing these various leadership styles over the years provided me with the wisdom and knowledge I needed to develop a style that works for me.

If you are in leadership, you have to ask yourself, "Is anyone following me?" If your answer is no, you have to ask yourself, "Why not?" Because without followers, you really aren't a leader. For a while, no one was following me because I couldn't let go. I would take control over everything because I didn't trust people. I didn't feel like they could do it my way. After hearing my team complain, become frustrated, and even quit in some instances, I learned I had to pull back and trust they would get it done, even if it was not exactly how I would have done it. I put them in position for a reason and had to give them the space to grow.

As a leader, it is my job to be a teacher, counselor, disciplinarian, cheerleader, motivator, and problem solver. I have to know when and how to adjust my leadership style. The truth is, you need to lead people in different ways if you are going to be effective.

If you are currently in leadership, my question to you is, "Are you motivated to lead?" Everyone wants a leader to lead and give direction. We have to position ourselves as a predictable, consistent resource they can count on for this leadership. We must hold our employees/team accountable and don't make other people's problems our own. You have enough of your own problems, so taking ownership of theirs will cause you to become stagnated and consumed with things you shouldn't be carrying. If you do have an employee or a team member who is not in line with your mission or culture, let that person go. You must remove the bad seeds —

or people who are just the wrong fit — as quickly as possible.

People are always watching you work. They are watching what you do as a leader and often model it, whether it's good or bad. If I'm expecting people to work hard and come in early, they need to see me doing just that. If it's my company, they need to see me working hard and doing the things that I expect from them, but they also need to see the balance. They need to see me stop working when I have to go, and care about how others feel. The rule of "treat people how you want to be treated" applies here, but it's also "do as you want those that follow you to do." I have to behave in the manner that I want my team to behave.

Supporting cast

In any given week, I receive a number of inquiries from individuals wanting to know if LIQUID SOUL is hiring and what it is that I look for when evaluating prospective team members. As a leader, I look for certain characteristics when seeking new talent. I look for people that have passion to learn. I look for drive and a competitive spirit to win. I look for someone who is not afraid to work hard, have fun, be honest, and speak their mind in a respectful way.

I look for someone smarter than I am in a specific area, a person who can be humble and realize he or she doesn't know it all. I want a person who is a problem solver and not a complainer. I want a thinker who doesn't just do what he is told but has the confidence to speak his mind if he feels a situation should be handled differently.

The ideal supporting cast member understands your business capabilities, knows exactly what you are selling, and can plug into those areas and do it well. People pay for expertise because it's sellable.

As a leader, you must know what you're talking about and represent the brand you're serving well. Remember that the team you assemble won't do it the same way you do it. Each person is unique, so you must be able to embrace individual differences. The key to good leadership is to make everyone of your staff members feel like a valued someone; and always hire people who know how to do things you can't. There's no need to hire your clone. You're only as good as those around you, and by surrounding yourself with smarter people, you become better.

I've hired the "fake it 'til you make it" types. Some have said they were experts in the area of project management or public relations. Some have professed to have a plethora of relationships that will help them excel in their new role; but when I gave them a chance, I quickly saw they didn't know anyone, had no public relations skills, and couldn't manage a project at all.

If you apply for a job at my firm and lie about your expertise, you will be found out very soon. We can see through smoke and mirrors. If a potential employee honestly admitted to a lack of experience — but showed some potential — I could make an informed decision to hire that person. I could help such an employee navigate, learn, grow, and augment his or her burgeoning skill set.

Our employees or our team members are critical components to stability, especially for entrepreneurs. I am a member of the 100 Black Men of Atlanta, and one of my mentors within the group said it to me best.

"Nick, I let my employees know, if I can't go off and play golf each Friday, why are you here?"

This means employees need to show their value. They must help lift some of the weight from the owner's back to allow him or her to do other things. If this is not happening, do they truly serve a purpose that is fostering the growth of their leader and the business?

Circle of trust

In life and in business, trust is extremely important. Through trial and error I've learned there is a process required to reach trust. People have to 'know' you and 'like' you before they can 'trust' you. Once people know who you are, and begin to like you, the natural progression from there is building trust. The benefit of this cycle is that once trust is established, real intimacy in relationship can begin. Within this intimacy, friendships and long-term business relationships are formed.

Remember the hilarious comedy "Meet the Parents," a tale of male nurse Greg Focker (Ben Stiller) who spends the weekend at the home of his girlfriend's parents and has to deal with her nightmare father, played by Robert De Niro? You will recall how part of poor Greg's stress is about being allowed into The Byrne Family Circle of Trust.

When it comes to our relationship circle, we should be in the center and the only other people around us should be those people who are the closest to us, and with whom we share unquestionable trust. We then have various 'circles' of trust within the circle, thus reflecting the degree of closeness and trust you have with various people in your life.

Just because someone is in your life doesn't mean they should be in your circle. In order to be inside your circle, a person should consistently have your basic trust. There shouldn't be anyone in your inner circle with whom you don't have a mutually fulfilling relationship based on love, care, trust and respect. No exceptions.

Decide who is worthy of your friendship. For years, I didn't take advantage of that because I didn't trust people. The tolls of being picked on as a child because of my weight and trying to fit in with the crowd as I got older, unbeknownst to me, had left a scar. I didn't love me, so how could I love someone else? I had let myself down in the past and therefore, I had trust issues with myself, which made trusting others quite difficult.

Overtime I've learned to get beyond my trust issues, because now I have a process of elimination when it comes to my circle. I have to know you, like you, and then trust you; but the truth is, not everyone may make it to the trust stage.

When you know you can have conversations with someone that won't leave the room, you are operating in trust. Family doesn't always fall into the trust area. Just because you are of the same family descent or relation doesn't give you a free pass to that area of my life. Like anyone else, you have to earn it.

We must identify who is worthy of our friendship and make a determination that we will do what it takes to be friends. Remember, God puts people in your life for a reason, a season or a lifetime. No matter what the length of time, we should do our very best to be in good relationships with them.

STAY TUNED TAKEAWAYS

- Be careful how you treat others. Avoid being selfish in relationships by carrying your weight and being a team player.

- Leaders must lead. If you don't have followers, you are not a leader.

- If someone desires to be in relationship with you, ask yourself why. Use discernment to understand their motives.

- In relationships, it's less about "me" and more about "we."

- Before letting someone into your inner circle, you must know, like and trust them.

Nick F. Nelson

Channel Seven

CHARITY STARTS AT HOME
Give where it counts most

The phrase "Charity starts at home" expresses the overriding demands of taking care of one's self and family before caring for others outside the family. The notion that a man's family should be his foremost concern is expressed in 1 Timothy 5:8, which says:

"But if anyone does not provide for his relatives, and especially for members of his household, he has denied the faith and is worse than an unbeliever."

As leaders or contributors to our households, we must understand before we can give to any organization, project, or business we're a part of, we have to give to our families. If I'm so tired that when I get home, I find myself falling asleep as soon as it hit the couch, then it means I'm giving too much energy to the wrong things.

What about your friend

Over the years, I've learned my marriage is the number one relationship I need to pay attention to and that my wife, Tiffany, should always be my priority. At one point in my professional career, work was my daily priority. My conversation at home would be about my day and the business. I didn't engage with her consistently about personal matters, nor did I even ask about her day.

Through time, experience and more mistakes than I can count, I've learned to change my actions, attitude and conversation. I find things to talk about other than work. Things that interest her and make it clear that nothing, including the business, is more important than she is.

As is the case with many married couples, Tiffany and I have had our fair share of disagreements. Sometimes they would occur because I was not transparent about my feelings regarding a specific subject, and it would be evident in my disposition, body language, and overall conversation. I would get frustrated, she would too, and a disagreement would ensue.

I had gotten so far off track that I was making my daily schedule as if I was the only one it affected. I was not consulting her on matters. I would simply tell her, "I have to go out of town" or "I have to attend an event tonight." Her response began to be, "You have to?"

After a while, it hit my spirit that my priorities were off. No, I didn't have to go, but I wanted to go. And if it really was urgent, I needed to make arrangements to fill the gap. Bottom line, I had to realize she had a schedule, too. So before I made plans, I needed to consult with her. I needed to know what was on the household schedule and determine where I might need to step in and if her schedule accommodated me going anywhere.

My client may want me to go to L.A. for three days, but what's going on at home may not accommodate that. Whenever I left, a void would be left open; yet, selfishly, I automatically assumed Tiffany would just always be there to fill it. I didn't realize the negative impact my schedule had on our home life. At the end of the day, she's my wife, not my maid, not an administrator nor a babysitter, but my wife.

I also had to realize I couldn't put Tiffany on the back burner and just expect her to cater to my schedule because the business or other people needed me. The truth is she needed me more.

Marriage can be difficult, and there may be times when you have to go back and remember why you got married in the first place. However, once you remember, you must then do what's required to sustain not only your marriage but also your friendship.

Parental guidance is suggested

As a youth leader in my church, I minister to children of all ages and with all types of family situations. Throughout my experience in working with children, and during my now eight years of raising my own child, what I've learned is that parental involvement is critical to a child's success.

I am very much aware that we live in a day and time where the nontraditional household is not so nontraditional anymore. Households with one parent, no parents or even grandparents rearing children have become commonplace. With an estimated 40 to 50 percent of marriages ending in divorce, the ones who suffer most are the children. I don't care if you are divorced or not, you must figure out a way to make your relationship work for the children.

A friend was sharing with me recently how he and his ex-wife chose to remain cordial, even chose to share the same home, in an effort to keep the family unit together. Now, I understand this situation will not work for everyone; however, if you are divorced with children, I encourage you to figure out how to make the relationship work so you can stay engaged in their lives.

Power in being present

Today, kids have any number of devices to keep them distracted; but that does not make up for a lack of a parent's presence. For families to stay tuned and connected with each other, all parties must be present, and this includes the kids, too. You need to set a "No devices" time to make sure everyone is engaged with one another.

A family benefits when members take time to stop, remove all distractions, and talk. As soon as I walk in the door each day, I ask my son, "How's it going?" This is my opportunity to connect with him and let him know I'm interested in what he does and reinforce with him that I'm always available for a father-child talk. I don't walk in the door with my cell phone to my ear anymore, giving him the impression he is second fiddle to my world outside the home.

Being present and tuned in with your spouse is equally important. You may not even have to ask, "How's it going?" If you are connected, you will know because you can read the answer through her tone of voice and body language.

When you are in tune, your spouse may say, "Yeah, I'm okay." But you will automatically "hear" that something is not right, because you know what "I'm okay" normally looks like, and this may not be it.

Crucial conversations

As it relates to communicating with your spouse, be on the lookout for drive-by conversations.

You know those times when you or your spouse says something slick like, "Got home pretty late again last night, huh?" as you are both in the midst of doing something else or you are headed out of the home. If — or should I say "when" — you find this occurring, press pause and take a minute to use that time as an opportunity for constructive conversation.

Several years ago while in corporate America, I read a book, "Crucial Conversations," by Kerry Patterson, Joseph Grenny, Ron McMillan & Al Switzler. It spoke directly to the critical need for putting things out on the table, not in a confrontational way, but in a way that allows us to open up when the stakes are high.

Part of the problem is we avoid crucial conversations because we want to avoid confrontation. We choose not to address the issues so we will have "peace and quiet." However, by delaying the talk, you might get the quiet but you are not finding real peace. Having peace is living and loving as a family unit, as husband and wife. I don't want "peace and quiet." I want to have peace.

Many couples are on roommate status; but to find balance and peace and to get out of roommate status, each person must act like adults. Even when you have an argument, someone has to be the adult. There are going to be times when your spouse has to be the adult, and there are going to be times when you're going to have to be the adult.

Being an adult means when you get into an argument, someone has to humble himself or herself to give room to a solution. Everything gets figured out when at least one party can be calm and levelheaded. This means your desire to get something off your chest may not be realized. You have to sit there, listen, and not interrupt even if your partner seems to be interrupting you.

It's so easy to say, "You did this or you didn't do that." You soon find yourself volleying like a tennis match, going back and forth, tit-for-tat. You must understand this is not a sport, but a marriage. Tit for tat doesn't solve anything.

If you choose to be the adult, you must help to figure out a solution. Sometimes you have to leave your stuff out of the conversation, knowing that there will be another time and a place to address it. I'm not saying you don't address it at all; it just may not be the right time. This is when you sit back and you say,

"Alright, do you have anything else to say?" It's all about getting to resolution. Finally, when seeking resolution, you must hear verbal confirmation from your mate that the matter is indeed resolved in some form.

The answer to your question may not be "Yes." It may be "I guess so." If that's the case, take it!

Mind your family business

The one thing you don't want is for your family to resent your job, your business, or other things you're involved in, because those things are taking you away. If you find yourself having to be away from home extensively because of work, travel, or other obligations and it feels as if your family is responding like they are in competition for your time and attention, watch out. They may be harboring resentment.

As an entrepreneur, I caution others not to spend so much time working on the business to the point that your family resents it, especially if you want your child to one day take it over. That child may end up resenting the business because dad was never at home.

You may justify spending so much time with the business because it's there, not at home, where you find the most "success." The world loves you, right? The world can build you up, give you accolades, awards, make you feel like you're the man; but what did it actually cost you? I had to check myself and say, "If I never got another award or single recognition for the rest of my life, I'll be okay as long as I have my family and people who love me."

One Sunday evening as I was home doing dishes, my son was just sitting around in his pajamas, and I asked him, "Son, what was the best part of your weekend?"

He quickly responded: "Hanging out with you."

The day before, we had been together from sun up to sun down. I made the day all about him. I put my phone away, cleared my mind and on that day, there was nothing more pressing than my son's need to engage with me and me with him.

His response to my question was better than any award I could receive. Being there for my son, for my family, is what truly matters. I encourage you to recognize this, see the value, and remember to handle your family business first.

A place for mom

My mother suffers from Alzheimer's disease. I suspected she had the disease for a while, but I never really wanted to accept it. I remember her coming to my home for Thanksgiving several years ago and getting confused, forgetting which room was which. In retrospect, I should have seen that as the onset of her condition, but I didn't focus on it. I accepted what my father was constantly saying, "That's just how your mama is."

So I began to believe she was just forgetful. As time went on and my father's health began to decline, so much attention was paid to him, I never really took the time to address my mother's needs as the dementia was taking over her mind.

I started focusing on the fact that something was wrong several years later, but by that point, her illness had progressed to where she needed as much care as my father. Knowing what I know now about the disease, even if I had addressed my mother's condition earlier, I couldn't have stopped it because it's degenerative; but I might have been able to put things in place sooner to slow it down.

Caring for my mom has been a journey. The journey literally began the day after my dad's funeral. The tragedy of it all is we had to trick her into leaving the home she and my father shared for over 40 years.

I knew she couldn't stay by herself and decided the best option for her was to live with her sister, my Aunt Pollie, in Chicago. I thank my Aunt Pollie and the rest of my family to this day because collectively, they agreed to take mom in and care for her until I could develop a long-term plan for her care.

There aren't many days that mom doesn't ask, "When am I going home?" She is referring to her home in Ohio. Recently, she got so angry with me, which happens often, that she put all her stuff in a bag and said, "I'm getting out of here." She sat by the door, frustrated, waiting for me to take her home.

You see home for mom now is Georgia. After months of contemplating after Dad died and asking myself questions like "Where will she live?" and "Who can help take care of her?"

the solution came from Tiffany. She, knowing me best said, "Nick wherever mom lives, it needs to be close to us so I can get to her quickly if needed and so that it eliminates any excuses for you not to visit regularly because she needs to see your face."

After Tiffany helped me identify the where, we worked together to identify the who. That who would be Yolanda Sanders, Mom's "good girlfriend." Yolanda worked as a personal aide for my parents prior to my Dad passing. To our surprise she agreed to move from Columbus to Georgia to serve as Mom's caregiver.

Over time mom's dementia has progressed to Alzheimer's and she is now in a place that specializes in caring for her needs. I had to find a place for mom, not just physically but in my life in general. I always had a closer relationship with my dad than my mom. My dad and I were just so much alike. But going through this process, through my father's death and my mother's illness, now we do have a close relationship. She's my mom but the roles have reversed, and I'm caring for her now.

It's amazing the little things she remembers. She remembers my family, her home. She remembers the bed she and my father shared, which she calls her "round bed." No matter how much I tell her she lives somewhere else now, she is still connected to that home; and part of that, I believe, is because she never had a chance to say goodbye.

I realized it's important for us to have closure to move on to the next door that's opening, but it's difficult to see the next step if we're still tied to the last. My mother didn't have closure; therefore, she is still holding onto what was.

Many people are still holding onto the past — past hurts, challenges, obstacles, situations or just memories because they are familiar; but they have no benefit as far as where you are now or where you need to go.

Recently, I wasn't feeling well, but I pulled myself out of the bed and got in the car to drive over and bathe my mom. When I got there, she fought me. She refused to get in the shower.

"Why do I need to get in the shower? I'm fine! I don't need a bath," she said repeatedly.

Finally, I just walked away. Frustrated, I called my mother's sister, my Aunt Pollie, for advice because she has experience dealing with mom when she gets this way. What she reminded me of was simple, yet profound. "Change that channel! Your mom will be fine. We'll all be dead and gone worrying about her crazy a%$ and she'll still be here."

What my Aunt had expressed, as only as she could, was true. I had to control my thoughts and let go of that which I had no power to change. If mom doesn't bath today, she will tomorrow. It took me a long time to get there with mom, but once I did, it was liberating.

I had a realization. How I responded allowed the situation to get me angry. People who know me know that I don't like confrontation, fighting or arguing. That's just not my personality.

That day, my mom fussed with me and said hurtful things, like, "Don't touch me, you're not my son. I'm taking you to jail."

I had to remind myself that she is sick, and she's my mother. I also had to remind myself it was the disease and not her.

These experiences of navigating my mother's disease have shown me how to think clearly in the face of confrontation, remain calm, and "change that channel."

Prior preparation prevents...

One thing I give props to my dad for is making certain everything was in place to care for my mother before he passed away. He made sure she had retirement funds to assist with her living and medical expenses. He also left final instructions for me, which were as follows: "Don't sell my home. Take care of my wife," and "Do no less for your son than I did for you."

Through all of his sickness, my dad made the needed preparations and left detailed instructions to make sure his family was taken care of even after he was gone, and I respect him for that. I work hard to follow his wishes; and to this day, we still own his home, and his wife/my mom is being taken care of. And thanks to Tiffany, my son has been to more countries and has had more experiences already than most people do in a lifetime.

It's important to me that I manage my affairs as my father wanted, and that I leave a legacy. The things we do today determine what we are able to leave behind for our families. For me, I live for my last name, not for my first. The name Nick will fade away, but that last name Nelson lives on through my family.

STAY TUNED TAKEAWAYS

- Before giving yourself to the things of this world, you must first give to your family.

- Treat your wife as your helpmate — key word being "help," which is also needed from you.

- There's power in your presence and being present. Never underestimate the ministry of just showing up.

- Don't avoid crucial conversations. If an argument ensues, remember to think like a man but act like an adult.

- Manage your affairs to ensure your legacy lives on long after you are gone. Your last name is more important than your first.

Channel Eight

FLYING LESSONS

Tightrope walker

Knowing when it's time to take a leap of faith is crucial. You know the moment when you say, "I'm going to jump out the window and figure out how to fly on the way down." Sometimes you just have to take flight.

I remember going to the circus as a child and seeing the tightrope performer slowly walk with so much confidence across that tiny rope pulled tight between two poles. He knew a net had been placed directly below him, prepared to catch him if by any chance he missed a step and fell. What I've learned along my journey is that God is my net and He is not going to allow any bad thing to happen to me if I fall.

God will always catch you. Just have the courage to jump and the faith to fly. You see, faith is foundational. You must eliminate the fear that stands in the way, stops so many believers, and has even killed so many dreams. You cannot let fear kill your dreams.

You have to push forward and figure it out along the way. You can spend years waiting and contemplating instead of acting. You put all your energy into making the perfect business plan, but if you have neglected to do a client plan, it's all a waste of time. You can spend a lifetime worrying about all the things that could go wrong, when in reality, they may never go wrong.

So, if your goal is to fly, I have some simple advice for you: Don't look down. Once you look down, you'll see the distance to the ground and you risk allowing fear to stop you, especially if you are afraid of heights. But, if you aren't afraid to be elevated, and if you can focus your sight ahead of you and jump in the direction of the place you desire to go, you just might make it.

Now, you may not make it on the first attempt; but as long as you're consistent and confident, you'll get there. You may even bruise yourself a little bit, but you know what that pain feels like because you've had tumbles before. Yes, you will be taking a risk; but as the saying goes, "No risk, no reward."

What's unfortunate is that many of us have great talents but never bring them to fruition. We never soar. Some have a powerful intellect but don't use it in their work. Some have a great talent for music or sports but are inconsistent in their practice. Some are great "people-persons" but work alone.

Sure, you can prepare and study as much as you want before you jump, but the real lesson comes from taking the leap and finding yourself unable to turn back. At that point, your only choice is to fly.

The key is learning how to move closer to the goal you've set for yourself. It means stepping out on faith to do something you've never done or maybe something you thought was impossible or at least a stretch for you. By soaking up all the knowledge you can harness from all sources available, you are preparing yourself to take flight into an unknown territory.

The start of something good

My business partner, Tirrell Whittley, and I met at FAMU in the fall of 1992. We were both interested in becoming members of Alpha Phi Alpha fraternity and although we participated in interest sessions together, we never really spoke to one another until an unusual encounter at a party. During the FAMU homecoming of 1992, we attended the Gorilla Thriller, which was the biggest Alpha party of the year. We both wanted to be selected for the Alpha Phi Alpha pledge class of Spring 1993, and attending that party was, let's just say, strongly encouraged.

That night, I had more than my fair share of jungle juice; and earlier in the evening, I had stolen all the toilet tissue out of the ladies room and had begun selling it to them as they entered (don't ask).

Tirrell came and sat next to me laughing about my entrepreneurial venture. I know he thought it was crazy but ingenious at the same time. We talked and laughed the rest of that evening, and that would be the beginning of our friendship.

In 2001, Tirrell and I launched Liquid Soul Radio, strictly as a hobby. Tirrell was in charge of the website while I programmed the station. A year later, it had grown into an online streaming music service with over 20 channels of music. In addition to online radio, we partnered with music publishing company ASCAP Atlanta to host live concerts in the city. We also had a deal with XM Satellite radio where we produced a weekly show. In all of this activity, we were making absolutely no money. During that time, we noticed a heavy demand for graphic and web design services, especially amongst the faith-based audience. After we experienced business challenges that caused us to shut down the radio station, we decided to reinvent ourselves.

In 2003, we changed our name from Liquid Soul Radio to Liquid Soul Media. Our primary target was the faith-based community, helping pastors, clergy and others develop stunning websites and marketing collateral. We managed to put together a small team of friends and volunteers to work with us and we went to market.

Over the next five years, we began to refine the business model, moving away from churches and setting our sites on a new target, Hollywood.

Furniture shopping

In 2007, after successfully marketing a handful of films and television shows, we began to look for office space. Finally, in 2008, we moved from working in our homes to acquiring an entire building in Atlanta. All the while, I was still holding onto my 9 to 5 on the opposite end of town. The mere fact that Tirrell convinced me to commit to a lease on a building I couldn't even work out of at the time, to this day, is his best sales job. What's interesting is I never saw being an entrepreneur as my life. In fact, I call myself an accidental entrepreneur because I never aspired to own a business. That was Tirrell's dream.

One day, Tirrell asked me to take a ride with him. We left our newly acquired empty office and to my surprise, we arrived at Ikea to look at furniture. As we walked around looking at office furniture, Tirrell would see a desk and point to it, saying, "That's going to be my desk."

He continued to point at other things, saying, "That's going to be my chair, that's going to be my trash can." He did this until he had picked out furniture for the whole office. At first, I thought he was crazy. I thought, "Why is this guy picking out furniture we're not prepared to purchase?" What I didn't realize at the time was that he was "naming and claiming it."

Tirrell was calling out that which was to be. He was speaking it into existence. I'm reminded of that experience today when I walk into his office and see a few of those same pieces he pointed to over 10 years ago.

No excellence on the side

In 2008, after seven years of trying to maintain the act of balancing life at work, family, and LIQUID SOUL, I knew I had to quit. Trying to maintain a full-time job, while working my side business both day and night, had worn its welcome on all fronts. I couldn't perform at my best because I lacked focus.

Tirrell and I are both deacons and attend the same church. One day, after service, we found ourselves talking casually with our bishop about our fears and frustrations. He listened and then made a statement that pushed us out the window and allowed us to fly. "Deacons!" he said, "You can't be excellent in your spare time."

After I took a minute to process what he said, I knew I had to quit. I was ready to leap; however, before doing so, I had to make sure my wife, Tiffany, was on board.

Remember, my decisions are bigger than I am. When I asked her if it was okay for me to quit my day job and go full-time with LIQUID SOUL, to my surprise, she said, "I thought you would have left by now."

She was right. By that time, we had clients, a building, payroll, employees, and most importantly, money in the bank. I was still nervous about leaping. The reality was I had been practicing flying for a while. I committed myself to learning the art of the take-off and was ready to soar. The only thing missing was her "Yes." Once I got that, I was clear for take-off. Her support and belief in my dream (her "Yes") is the reason why I am an entrepreneur to this day.

Doing something that doesn't make you happy is like being caged in a cell. Ask yourself what things are binding you, thereby holding you back from being free? Why are you self-conscious? Are you scared of the change you need to make?

It could be relationship challenges or maybe you have a hard time trusting people because of past hurts. You must identify those things and attack them with all you have inside.

Sure, change can be difficult, but you could be overstaying your welcome. When it's time to go, you have to go. You have to relinquish fear because it will hold you back from manifesting so many great ideas that will never see the light of day because you are afraid to act.

I was liberated when I realized that corporate America would always be there. I had the skills to find another job but only one opportunity to take the open window and create a path for myself before that window closed. We are given windows of opportunity in life. You have a choice when you see it open:

You either jump through or allow it to close on you. I chose to jump out of that open window and explore my entrepreneurial path, but it wasn't easy.

Dinks (dual income no kids) no more

Once Quinn was born, I could immediately see the connection that was forming between him and Tiffany. I could also sense her priorities beginning to shift. Even before Quinn was born, Tiffany had mentioned to me that it was not her desire to work and that God was calling her to do something greater. Now of course this scared me to death because we were DINKS and had all of the luxuries and expenses that came along with the title.

After weeks on maternity leave, the day we both dreaded had finally arrived. Quinn's first day of day care. Tiffany, to my surprise, did very well. As to be expected, tears were shed, but we both had faith that things would work out, and they did for some time.

Months went by and we began to adjust to our new life. One area that was tough for me was my work schedule. At the time I hadn't made the transition full-time to LIQUID

SOUL and was still working for UPS. Well, those of you who have ever worked for "Big Brown" understand that there can be a "get there early and stay late" culture. As a result, most days Tiffany bore the burden of picking up Quinn. She had asked if I could shift my schedule and quite frankly I probably could have, but I didn't want to because I was one of a very few black managers with a team and did not want my work ethic questioned.

Over time, the issue of my work schedule was becoming more and more of a problem. Even after I left UPS months later, the issue of my schedule and me supporting Tiffany sufficiently with our newborn son persisted. She had a demanding job, as well, yet I acted as if my demands were greater. Something had to give.

After giving me her "yes" to my leaving corporate America, Tiffany asked that I do the same regarding her desire to quit her job and become a full-time mom. It was 2009 and I was now working LIQUID SOUL full-time; and given Tiffany's desire to fulfill her calling and me working long hours trying to grow the business, we both knew this was the right thing. I was still scared. The financial burden would be all on me and I would have no choice but to make my business work.

Fast forward eight years later. Tiffany is still at home and we have been able to maintain our lifestyle. Yes, it has required some sacrifices, but the benefits far outweigh them. Our son, Quinn, has the benefit of having Tiffany at home to help reinforce what he's learned in school, to ensure he truly understands. Our church has the benefit of having a full-time youth leader in Tiffany, who has been able to take the ministry to the next level and has helped pour into the lives of a countless number of children. I have the benefit of having a support system to help me balance the craziness that can be my life. Through it all God has received the benefit to his kingdom because we stepped out on faith and did not let fear stop us.

I've gotta do what I gotta do

Creating marketing strategies and executing them was my comfort zone at LIQUID SOUL. That's what I had done since its inception and was what I knew. In 2013, after a tough year, I was asked to help with finding new business opportunities. Selling was not my thing. I'm the background guy that creates the ideas, manages the staff and gets the work done. That was my mentality. After more discussions, I realized if I am to be a partner in this business, I have to do what is required, not just what I'm comfortable doing. This experience taught me that if you're in business, you always have to be selling something. It's great if you have the luxury to hire others, but if not, you have to go out there and get the business yourself. It's not always about planning and strategy, but action is a key component of all success.

I had to learn the art of sales by asking questions to find my style. I had tried hard to stay in my lane before, but that wasn't being a team player. The team needed more from me at that moment.

I had to be real with myself, and say, "Nick, you're not carrying your weight. If you're going to do this, which you profess to love, you can't accept just one piece; you have to accept all of it, and sales and financials are a part of it." It's not just the areas in which you feel comfortable; it's all about being prepared to do everything that helps the business succeed.

Running a business means finding clients. If you don't have clients, you're not in business. I've seen so many entrepreneurs focus on the work and forget the clients. Here is a classic scenario: Business is coming in but they stop selling. It happened to us with LIQUID SOUL. We had so much word-of-mouth business that we spent more time working than selling. It was fun and we had a passion for helping our clients. But, we forgot we needed to sell. We had to keep customers coming in. Once our projects were completed, we realized there was little in our pipeline and found ourselves scurrying to secure and close deals to keep the business going.

It was up to me to step up to the plate and force myself to get into sales. I had to push and motivate myself by saying, "Nick, you can do this! It's not rocket science!"

I had the case studies and examples. This was my business and I understood every aspect of it. Now, it was time to for me to sell our success. I had to position myself and our company to win. It was time to focus on the goal and go!"

The power of no

To achieve work-life balance, you have to avoid wasting time on opportunities that aren't there. Being an entrepreneur, I've mastered the art of identifying what's real as quickly as possible, to move to the next thing.

The fact of the matter is people will waste your time if you let them. You must be able to quickly assess if there's a real business opportunity. The longer you try to pursue something that really is not going to generate any additional business for you, the more you are losing money and time that could be spent on real business development activities.

Sometimes people are afraid of the word "no." Most hate hearing it, but I appreciate the word because what that "no" does is free me up to pursue something else that may be a viable opportunity, as opposed to wasting my time. In business and in life, when you realize certain things are not going to work, get to an answer of "no" as soon as possible.

If there is something you want to pursue, but it's not working right now, accept it. The key is knowing that a "no" now doesn't necessarily mean a "no" later; but also understand that when the answer is really "no," don't fool yourself that it might become a yes.

I pursued a consumer products company and its CEO strongly for months, but kept hearing, "Hey, I'm going to get back to you."

But "going to" and actually "doing it" are two different things. I made trips back and forth trying to preserve the deal, put presentations together, all in an effort to get the business. Ultimately, I never got a dime, and that hurt.

We made the mistake of counting the revenues that we were "going to receive" as a part of our projected budget. We did this because we were told on multiple occasions, "Yes, we're going to work with you guys, we want to work with you." Unfortunately, this potential client never signed an agreement.

Instead of saying, "We're just going to put this on the back burner, but when we're ready, we'll contact you," they said nothing. We were thinking, "Yes! It's a done deal," but we learned that it's never done until the contract is signed.

You have to be careful in those instances. You have to give yourself a threshold to know when it's time to back away. In business and in life, "no" is not a bad word; it could very well be the word you needed to hear.

The eagle and the chicken

When I started to work LIQUID SOUL full-time, I knew I had made the right decision because it didn't feel like work. I would, and still do, wake up every day excited to get to the office. This is because I made the decision to take control of my career.

This decision to jump out the window and fly has given me the ability to call the shots. It's catapulted me from a career in Information Technology to my dream career in advertising. It's taught me that the more we take control of our lives, the more options we have to establish balance. Too many of us have tunnel vision when we should have peripheral vision to be able to see our complete surroundings. We have to see the things from the front, but also from the side where they could be coming at you.

I knew I wanted more out of life. I wanted to use my gifts and talents to create something new that would not only sustain my family but also provide the freedom I sought. I knew I wasn't created to spend my life tied to a desk being told what to do; I wanted to use the skills I had to create something innovative. A friend's dream, a pastor's wisdom and a "yes" from my wife literally changed the entire trajectory of my life — something for which I am eternally grateful to each for providing.

When I think about my experience, I'm reminded of the fable of the hardworking farmer who found an eagle's egg lying on the grounds of his farm. He was in a hurry, so he didn't give much attention to it and quickly placed it in the chicken coop with all the chicken eggs. After a couple days, the egg hatched, and the eagle was born.

The eagle looked around and assumed he was a chicken, so the eagle clucked and pecked and dug for worms. He scurried about and occasionally jumped around, flying a few feet in the air like the chickens. Over the years, the eagle grew old and tired. One day, he saw a magnificent bird flying overhead with grace, skill, and profound beauty. The bird was unfettered as it glided through wind and rain across the sky.

"Who is that?" asked the eagle. "That's the king of the birds," replied a chicken, "The bald eagle! She is one with the sky. The sky is her home. We are chickens and our home is on the ground."

And so the eagle lived and died a chicken, for that's what he believed he was. For years, I was an eagle living like a chicken; however, I did not die in that position but took flight once I realized who I was, on the inside.

My question for you: Are you an eagle, too, but acting like a chicken?

STAY TUNED TAKEAWAYS

- Don't be afraid to step out on faith. If you take the first step, God will guide you the rest of the way. He won't let you fall.

- Speak the desires of your heart into existence. If God has given you a vision and has told you to move, then you move.

- Being excellent requires focus. You can't be excellent in your spare time.

- Step out of your comfort zone and step into something new that will challenge you.

- In business and in life, get to an answer of "no" as soon as possible. A "no" today can free you up to pursue actual opportunities tomorrow.

PHYSICAL THERAPY
(BALANCING ACT)

The secret to work-life balance

Closing your eyes and picture this: You are standing in one side of a scale; and on the opposite side, you see all the things that are currently adding to your daily load. Ask yourself, "Am I equipped with all that I need to handle what's before me?"

Don't worry. You don't have to keep that kind of scale balanced. Work-life balance does not mean an equal balance. Trying to schedule an equal number of hours for each of your various work and personal activities is usually unrealistic. Life is, and should be, more fluid than that.

Despite a growing worldwide quest, work-life balance still eludes most. Many of us don't know how to begin to accomplish this.

Some say they want it but aren't actively seeking it. Still others are so lost that they have thrown their hands up and have chosen to go with the flow and just hope for the best. My own experience has taught me one thing for sure: As long as you don't have a plan, balance is just a pipe dream.

I love to run; and about a year ago, I was advised to see a physical therapist to help relieve some tendinitis issues I was experiencing. The therapist asked me to do a number of exercises. One exercise in particular changed my life, as it revealed to me the secret to achieving work-life balance.

In this exercise, you have to hold your arms out to your side to create a T with your body. Next, you hold one leg up and do your best to stand on the other and balance. I tried this exercise once; and when I raised my right leg and began balancing on my left, I began to sway to my right side heading for a fall. All I could do to stop myself from falling was to put down the foot that was raised. I repeated this exercise several times and each time had to put my foot down to maintain my balance. After about the fourth time performing it, the

Holy Spirit revealed to me the lesson therein. That lesson is that to achieve balance in my life, I would have to put my foot down. If I was going to prioritize my life and find balance, I needed to start using words and phrases like: "No," "I can't do it," and "I don't have time today."

Swatting flies

I recently read a news story about a woman who was driving and lost control of her car. She hit a guardrail before the car flew off the road, plunged down a cliff, rolled down an embankment, and landed in a creek. It's amazing she survived.

A stranger who saw the accident happening came to the rescue of the elderly driver.

"The vehicle landed on its wheels, which was a great thing," said a State Patrol spokesman. "It only rolled one complete time, so that's pretty good."

Rescuers used the "Jaws of Life" to cut the elderly woman out of the crumpled car. She walked away from the wreck with minor injuries. We can all learn a lesson from this crash, and that is to avoid any distractions while driving. The investigators explained she was swatting at a fly, and that caused her to lose control.

The moral of the story is to recognize distractions in your life before they cause you to veer off course and crash. For years, I was like the woman who lost control of her car. I was swatting at flies daily. I was easily distracted because there was always something vying for my attention; and I would oblige no matter if it happened by chance or deliberately by shifting my focus and taking my eye off the road. In order for me to maintain balance in my life, I've learned I have to focus, prioritize and eliminate distractions.

Give yourself permission to stop

We often think we have to do everything. We pile a lot on our plates and none of it gets done or done well. We become overwhelmed because we haven't given ourselves permission to stop. It's important to identify and understand those things that have to be done today. Once you have completed those priorities, everything else is extra credit.

When we stop, we have an opportunity to make sure we're implementing quiet time as a part of our day. You can use that quiet time to reflect and analyze vital issues, and to ask yourself, "Who am I?" "What am I supposed to be doing?" "Who do I need to have in my life?" and "What do I need to let go of?"

This is your vision-setting and assessment time. My time is usually around 5 a.m. at the gym while I have background tunes in my ear.

Until recently, I took a great sense of pride in being able to function without much sleep. You've heard people say, "I stayed up all night grinding, I'm down with #teamnosleep." "Can't stop, won't stop." Or "Tired rhymes with fired."

I heard them all and embraced the concept before I grew wiser and realized I needed my sleep. During those wee hours in the morning while sitting at the computer, I was much less productive. A better use of my time was actually sleeping.

My lack of sleep and quiet time caught up with me recently, and it was clear something needed to change.

"Dad, wake up!" my son (who, by the way, gets his 8 to 12 hours of sleep) yelled.
Each evening, our routine is for me to spend time with him either playing a video game or watching his favorite television program. Because of my lack of sufficient sleep, there were days I was so exhausted I couldn't even keep my eyes open with toothpicks.

My son wants to hang around Dad, but what good is having me there if I'm asleep 5 minutes after sitting down? I realized I had to start getting to bed early. I could no longer substitute coffee, 5-Hour Energy, or B12 for the one thing my body was craving the most.

I work in Atlanta but live about 45 minutes outside of the city in the suburbs. Many days, I find myself driving home late and feeling exhausted. Candidly, there have been times when I have been too tired to get behind the wheel. Some nights, I'd arrive at home, pull in my driveway, and have no memory of the full commute.

As an entrepreneur trying to balance business, family, and other personal responsibilities, sleep was a luxury that I often felt I just could not afford. I remember years ago when my business partner and I were trying to start LIQUID SOUL and I was still working in corporate America. I had no extra time. During the day, I would meet the demands of my job that paid the bills and in the late evenings, I'd pursue my dream.

Years later, these same bad habits of working late in the evenings, getting up early to work out and taking care of personal business still existed; and it was literally killing me. I knew I had to make a change for sure after I reviewed a report, produced from my activity tracker, which showed just how little sleep I was getting. It read that on average, I was getting approximately 3 hours of sleep each night within any given week. When I saw this, I was alarmed, especially considering the Centers for Disease Control (CDC) recommends 7-8 hours of sleep each night for adults.

Now, did I realistically feel I could achieve that goal? Well, no. However, I knew I could do better than 3 hours per night.

I've come a long way. Today, I take pride in being a relatively healthy guy. I eat reasonably, work out, monitor my blood pressure, and take my vitamins daily. I do all of the things that a person seeking to be healthy is supposed to do.

I'm still not getting sufficient sleep, but I am setting a course for changing that. I see the lack of sleep affecting my blood pressure and the hypertension that I am managing through prescription medication. Now, of course, it's not my desire to stay on medication forever. So what can I do to get off the meds? Sleep!

You would think that alone should be a good reason for me to want to lie down. Lack of sleep also affects memory and cognitive behavior. Whether we are talking about directions or names, I've always struggled in this area. Weight is another area in which I've struggled, and sleep plays a role here, too. You actually burn calories when you sleep. Also, if you're asleep, you're not tempted to go for that bowl of ice cream, cookies, or any other craving that may call you in the wee hours of the morning.

Take back the remote

Sometimes we let life's daily scenarios consume us, causing us to lose our minds. If we consistently allow that to happen, we'll be no

good to anyone. On any given day, employees may be requiring a lot of my time, clients may have unreasonable requests, or my mom may be having a rough day with her Alzheimer's disease.

That's just my reality. However, I cannot allow it to stand in the way of accomplishing what's before me. If I find myself feeling consumed with life, I have to recognize it and get control of my thoughts before they negatively affect my actions.

I call this taking back the remote.

Remember our decisions affect at least three to four people around us. My responsibility to others is bigger than my need to wallow in self-pity that adds no value to my life. Instead of wallowing in self-pity or going crazy, I have to find quiet time. I have to be still and hear God's voice to be rejuvenated. That's part of taking care of you — your core being — giving yourself permission to rest and rekindle through sleep.

If something is aching, I urge you to get it checked out; don't wait. It's up to you to take care of the one and only you that you have. So figure it out. Do what you need to do. It's not a matter of WHETHER you can succeed; rather, it's a matter of WHEN.

How do you take back the remote, or in other words, take your life back? You take your life back by recognizing and understanding all the steps that I've shared in this book.

There's something in the fraternity world called reclamation. When you reclaim a brother, you get something back that had been lost. This may be a relationship, an opportunity, your focus, your vision, or a dream. All the things you've broken along the way can be repaired, and what's been lost can be found when you make a conscious decision to stay tuned and reclaim your life.

The shift that changed my life was realizing that I was my own worst enemy. For most of my life, I've struggled with self-identity. I didn't really know who I was and had accepted what I had been called or what others saw me as. I was allowing others to take control of my life, which was easy because I wasn't controlling it myself. I was giving up the remote control without a fight whatsoever.

After my dad and my pastor, who reintroduced me to church, passed away, things were tough. I felt like my wings had been clipped and I couldn't find my balance. They had been my wise counsel. They were the men in my life whom I called my sounding board, and now they were both gone and I felt alone. My norm had been disturbed and my core had been shaken. But I soon realized the Ds of Life can build you or break you all the way down, depending on how you carry them.

The wake-up call in life is equivalent to setting more than one alarm on your phone: If you really want to ensure you wake up, it's advisable to set multiple alarms.

As life progressed, multiple alarms went off at different times, and eventually I got it. To tune in, I had to loosen the chains that were keeping me bound: chains of self-consciousness; chains of not knowing who I was; chains of not setting boundaries; and chains of allowing anyone to do anything to me that I did not sanction.

Setting boundaries for your life can save you on multiple levels. The reason we sometimes fail is that we don't set boundaries. Sometimes it's not until you push the limits that you realize where the boundaries are -- and when to go past them. If you're wise, you'll recognize change is necessary.

In order to change, you must first be real with yourself and say, "I need to change." The next step is answering the following five key questions:

1. For whom am I changing?
2. What does change look like in my life?
3. When is change necessary?
4. Why is change important?
5. How do I sustain that change?

I was recently asked, "What's the true benefit of change?"

The answer for me is "peace." Every person should strive to have internal peace rather than internal conflict. You must work to remove the chains that keep you bound, because each broken chain brings you closer to your peace. To secure my peace, I had to break chains of addiction, insecurity, obesity, and lack of control, to name a few. Each broken chain has brought me closer to peace.

What is true peace? Peace is a feeling of contentment, of feeling okay even when you don't have it all together.

Rapper Kendrick Lamar has a song entitled "Alright," where he declares no matter what challenges he has in life, "It's gone be alright!" That's peace.

I may not have all the answers, but that's okay. I may have bad days and feel like quitting, but that's fine. Maybe I haven't reached my goals yet, but it's cool. I've learned to accept the things that I cannot change and be okay with that. I've learned to find peace where I am right now and not go crazy in the meantime.

Understanding what you need to do and where you want to go will help you internalize the process for, and prompt you to act on, your change. I realized many of my problems stemmed from not being tuned in. I therefore had to put parameters in place in every area I needed to tune in, and I made sure I was becoming the leading man I desired to be.

Sometimes, we are afraid to let go of the past and who we have been; but we can overcome that by having a mindset that everything really is going to be okay. Accept that people do things differently and we all make mistakes, but it will be okay. If I lose a client, another one will come along, and it will be okay. I've adopted that mindset in my life and it has changed my entire outlook.

I truly had to explore my reason for the change I envisioned. To tap into my why and follow my purpose, I had to maintain my focus. I had to start disengaging in certain areas of my life in order to focus on the priorities and overcome the hurdles that had the potential to derail me.

I've identified my lane, I'm running in it, and I make it fun. With that said, change can be one of the most difficult things to sustain. I still have moments when I think about quitting, but I believe that happens to all of us. When I have those moments at work, for example, I've learned to trick my brain by saying, "Nick, you're only one or two deals away from the next level." Too often we stop, not realizing we're at the two-yard line. We could have made it to the end zone and won the game but instead we let time run out because we quit too soon. Winning is truly about sustainability and finishing the drill.

Take back the remote control in your life and take charge of all aspects, from your health to your relationships, to your money, to everything else. You must work one by one, putting Humpty Dumpty back together again and getting the pieces back in focus; then prioritize to stay in focus by understanding and putting thresholds in place.

Set your sights on what you're interested in, and don't let other people dictate the pace of your life. There's nothing wrong with accepting advice; but beware of people who want to take control and tell you what to be, where to go and what to do. Only you and God can decide your best course of action.

STAY TUNED TAKEAWAYS

- To achieve work-life balance, you have to put your foot down. You must be decisive in determining your commitments.

- Recognize and then avoid those things that are distractions in your life. Concentrating on them will cause you to lose focus.

- Give yourself permission to stop. For you to be at your best, you need sufficient rest.

- Take back the remote control in your life by getting control of your thoughts and decision-making before they negatively affect your actions.

- Remove the chains that keep you bound. Only through their removal will you find peace and contentment.

Channel Ten

NEXT SEASON
Preparing for fall

Traditional broadcast television programming is broken into seasons. The term "fall launch" in TV terminology refers to the programing planned for debut in and around September. Other series launches are scattered throughout the remainder of the year.

The success or failure of television shows from one season to the next hinges on Nielsen ratings. Nielsen ratings are an audience measurement system, owned by Nielsen Company, used to determine the audience size and composition of television programming in the United States. The shows that receive satisfactory ratings tend to remain on air and in many instances are renewed for another season. Those that do not are canceled.

Another tool used by Nielsen Company to determine audience viewership is what it calls the "sweeps" period. Sweeps began in a simple era when everyone watched TV programs or shows on a real television tube rather than on laptops and phones. That refers to the period when everyone sat down to watch a show at the exact time it was aired, unlike today when we have many video on-demand options available.

Nielsen would send "TV diaries" to households across America, asking viewers to record their precise TV viewing habits for a week. Then, in a geographic "sweep," starting in the Northeast and moving to the West, Nielsen would collect the booklets, compile the data, and publish the accurate reports on the viewing habits of American families.

You may be asking, "What does this have to do with me finding work-life balance and peace?" The answer is that we have to determine what season of life we're in so that we can take measurements and determine ratings in all areas of our lives.

Imagine the impact if you surveyed the people in your life to determine your effectiveness.

What if you received feedback that helped you improve your shortcomings and deliver the content your viewers wanted, which would ultimately help you succeed and or improve your ratings? Sometimes a quarterly sweep or pulse check may be just the thing needed to make sure you're prepared for and are headed in the right direction to make the most of it.

Assessing your success

As with the ratings, we have to assess how we did in the previous season to determine our strategy for the current and potential future seasons. This is where most of us miss it. I missed the assessment stage for years. If I had been keeping up, I would have canceled the show that was running episodes about me several seasons ago. My picture had been so out of focus I couldn't see what was directly in front of me.

When we neglect to analyze and assess where we are right now in life, it's impossible to create effective plans to improve.

Our jobs use performance evaluations to assess us annually. At the conclusion of that evaluation, we typically set goals and objectives for the next period and, in some instances, a performance plan. I encourage you to set a performance plan of your own.

Continually working to improve your show and making it more compelling to drive ratings is how you secure your slot for the next season. This is how you position yourself for continued success. If we don't make a plan, we're taking a haphazard approach, and we appear clueless.

It's like someone saying, "I need to lose some weight and I'm going to get to it one day," "I'm going to," "I need to," "I want to ... but," or "I should."

These are the phrases we get stuck on that give us permission to continue to put things off and wait until the next season to do it, being oblivious to the fact that now is all we have. There is a song by the gospel group The Winans that says, "...tomorrow, tomorrow, I'll give my life tomorrow; I thought about today, but it's so much easier to say...tomorrow."

The song goes on to say, "Who promised you tomorrow? You better choose the Lord today, because tomorrow could very well be too late."

We all think we have so much time, but we don't. Life is not a dress rehearsal. This is the main act, and there are no retakes.

In this next phase of life, you must negotiate a new contract with yourself and the people you serve. You have to create and share multiple plans for tomorrow that will help make your "right now" balanced and peaceful; but you must act today.

Your plan for next season must include retirement, household/family, financial planning, career/business, and personal development. You're the writer, producer and director of your show. This is your vision. It's all about being present now, with a plan for your next season, based on the results of the last season.

We have to be forward thinking; we can't be so ingrained or in the weeds that we're not thinking ahead. For example, if you own a business, you have to understand what's going on with your current operations at the same time as you're creating a pipeline of new opportunities.

That is one of the biggest challenges small business owners face, as they are wearing multiple hats, trying to do the work, and selling the work at the same time. That may work for a season but it's hard to sustain. For long-term success, you need to grow your business by taking on the right work (not all work is good), get paid at the right price, and bring on the right people with the right spirit who can manage the details so you don't have to be overly engaged. That's the model responsible for LIQUID SOUL's success. That's how we've decided to grow so we can get to our next season.

The tilling, plowing, and planting for the next season must be on your terms without compromising you — it's all part of a balancing act. So what if you're successful (whatever that is) while you compromise you? So what if your family is okay but you compromise you? It's a problem, because if you compromise you, what you won't have is peace. Soon resentment will begin to set in because you're playing peace instead of actually possessing it. To have it in your life, you must stay tuned. You must be true to yourself.

Being renewed and future focused

As for my next season, the script is still being developed. I do know it includes helping others create balance in their career and personal lives similar to what I've had to do multiple times. That's the reason I even decided to write this book. I'm starting the plan for my next season right now.

I've determined I'm in the third quarter of life based on my age; that is, where I am now both personally and professionally, and where it is I have yet to go. Since I'm still in the third quarter, I have time to make adjustments if I'm not winning in a particular area. As to those areas in which I am winning, it's my job to protect the lead.

In order to get to the top, I need a foundation that can support a towering edifice. I want to help people be who they were created to be and walk in their purpose, which requires balance and peace. I understand that doesn't always come with a check, so I have to hang in there, be obedient, act on God's direction, and wait in expectation for the result.

To get to that understanding, it took prayer, soul searching, mistakes, and doing exactly what I did when I started LIQUID SOUL. I had to create a strategy based on where I was, where I wanted to go, what I wanted to do, who I wanted to be, and the best way to become that person. I then had to broadcast my vision to the world.

Learn to see yourself as a gift. No matter what stage of life you're in, you always have something to give that will make someone's day better: a smile, a compliment, a hug, a listening ear, or space to merge into traffic. It doesn't have to be much to make a difference. Practice being a giver. When you do it well, it becomes less of what you do but more of who you are. The greatest, most influential people are the ones who use themselves as gifts to others.

Closing credits

I've spent a little over three years working on my next season by developing my personal brand, putting my toe in the water to gauge the temperature, and getting feedback from people. I read comments from my social media posts to determine what excited people by recognizing what they did or did not respond to. I've studied and explored ways I could be different and stand out in the crowd.

My survey of the landscape revealed there aren't many people providing knowledge and inspiration, being transparent about their lives and helping to motivate in ways that affect others, especially professional men, by providing clear and basic areas of knowledge around real life situations. I saw that as an opportunity for me.

Using the internet today, you can easily tell your story through blogs, videos, social posts, and other avenues. People see the information and pass it on. Today, it's about leveraging and taking advantage of available tools, about being proactive and determining where you want to go.

You should always be evolving, learning, and growing; and never stay stagnant, as comfort can become your worst enemy. Ask yourself how you can improve, and remember that making great decisions is important to this process. Before making any decisions, take a moment to think about how your decision affects others.

My next step is where my blessing is, so I must identify how to get to it. This is necessary because I'm not complacent; I desire to have more, and I'm determined to get it.

Tiffany and I celebrated our 16th year of marriage this year. I thank God for her love and support over the years, even in those times when I might not have deserved it. My eyes are wide open. I know what life is about. It's about enjoying and living every single day to its fullest because tomorrow is never promised. It's about discovering how to make our families and those around us better.

I recently had a conversation with a friend who reminded me that in 10 years our son will be out of the house and it'll just be Tiffany and I. It made me think about how to maximize these remaining years with my son and soak up every moment, because in the blink of an eye he will be grown.

I've learned from the lessons and shortcomings of my father and my pastor, and I thank them for that. They gave me the gift of their lives as a testament and an example of what I should and shouldn't do. Although my father was brilliant in all of his studies, teachings, and travels, he struggled to effectively find balance. And although my pastor had an awesome amount of wisdom, he did not follow sage advice on his health, which might have prolonged his life. My father and my pastor were not only my life examples of true manhood, but also they were my wake-up call.

In life, things and events are happening continuously, both positive and negative — maybe you are going into, are in, or are coming out of a storm. You need to know what season you're in to have an idea of what to expect, and acknowledge and prepare for the next one on the journey. These seasons include events or acts that are flip sides of each other: birth and death; plant and uproot; gather and scatter; keep and throw away; repair and tear; speak up and be quiet; find and lose; build up and tear down; heal and kill; laugh and cry; love and hate; dance and grieve; and, finally, peace and war.

Just like a television show, know that you are being viewed and rated by others while you go through the seasons of your life; but you also must view and rate yourself.

The Bible tells us, in Ecclesiastes 3:1, there is a time for everything and a season for every activity under heaven. We are rated and judged by those on earth and our Father in heaven. How you respond and the results you have will determine if you'll be renewed for another season.

So, how do you prepare for your next season? You pray, plan, practice, and perfect the steps I've shared in this book. Whatever season you are in, you must keep an open dialogue with God and ask Him to order your steps to get through.

I have a great expectation for more from my marriage, my mother and her well-being, my business, my finances, my son, my community and my life as a whole. I want more, and there is no reason I can't have more. I'm driven to create the balance. Instead of falling asleep in front of the TV, I'm taking back the remote, turning it off, getting up off the couch, and focusing on creating more memories and influencing even more lives —

and I'm starting with my family. At the end of the day, that's my why. Stay tuned.

"Beeeeeeeeeeeeeeeeeep"

STAY TUNED TAKEAWAYS

- We live life in seasons. It's important to understand what season of life you are in so that you can respond accordingly.

- Take the time to analyze and rate your performance in all areas of your life. For those areas that require improvement, develop a plan to change.

- Don't assume you have tomorrow to accomplish a goal. Release the temptation to put things off.

- Be forward thinking. Plan for the future before you get there.

- Expect more from life. Don't remain stagnant, but instead evolve and seek new opportunities and new blessings for your next season.

CPSIA information can be obtained
at www.ICGtesting.com
Printed in the USA
LVOW04s1322081016

507901LV00002B/3/P